Relative Connections

Dedication

To mom, the person who gave all of us a passion for creativity and words.

Relative Connections

F. Sharon Swope

Genilee Swope Parente

Allyn M. Stotz

Christina Rae Parente

Mark A. Swope

This novel is a work of fiction. Any references to real people, events, establishments, organizations or locales are intended only to give the fiction a sense of reality and authenticity, and are used fictitiously. All other names, characters and places, and all dialogue and incidents portrayed in this book, are the product of the authors' imaginations.

An e-book edition of this book was published in 2018 by GSP Publishing.

Relative Connections. Copyright © 2018 by GSP Publishing. All rights reserved. Printed in the United States of America. No part of this book may be used or reproduced in any manner whatsoever without written permission except in the case of brief quotations embodied in critical articles and reviews.

For information contact:
GSP Publishing
www.swopeparente.com
swopeparente@gmail.com

Dear Readers,

People are connected in infinite ways: circumstances, coincidence, profession, need. All of us, however, begin life connected to a bloodline. The authors of this book of short stories are related by blood.

In our family, we credit our love of reading and writing to the matriarch of our clan: F. Sharon Swope, who believed that a good place for her growing children to spend their leisure time was between the pages of a book. She taught all of us to love trips to the library and hours spent absorbing the words of stories, then turning what we read into images in our mind.

The reach of her lessons went beyond the authors featured here to include all her children, grandchildren and great-grandson. Even those who did not write a story specifically for this book have developed this passion for words.

The stories in this collection talk about making connections not just to our own relatives, but to those we make family despite the fact our DNA does not match. That includes new and old friends, the animals we come to love, the lovers who touch our lives.

We hope that our words will inspire you to stop and take the time to appreciate the people and pets that come to mean so much to you.

Sincerely,

Genilee Swope Parente

Table of Contents

Fleeing the Nest.......................... 13
  F. Sharon Swope

Adventures with Heroes 37
  Genilee Swope Parente

The Gift Box................................ 61
  F. Sharon Swope

Different Seats........................... 85
  Genilee Swope Parente

Shedding Her Skin.................... 107
  F. Sharon Swope

Twinkles from Heaven 129
  by Allyn M. Stotz

One in the Bush 149
  Genilee Swope Parente

Dream Date 177
Christina Parente

A Friend Comes Home 191
Mark Swope

The authors 212

Fleeing the Nest

F. Sharon Swope

The driver put his giant bus in reverse and backed out of the parking slot. Sophie Blackwell let out a huge sigh of relief. *I've done it. I've really done it.*

Four years of planning and saving money hadn't been easy given the fact she didn't work outside the home. Her family had discouraged it. "You're too small and vulnerable," was a constant refrain from her brothers, her dad, her uncle and most of her cousins. "It's dangerous and we can't be out there to take care of you." They seemed to think she had everything she needed right there on the farm. They used the same excuse to discourage her from moving away to attend college, though Sophie suspected part of the truth was the farm had fared too poorly to provide money for further education.

She was sick of hearing how defenseless and diminutive and vulnerable she was just because she was the only woman on the farm—dwarfed by the giant, strong men who worked the land. She started stashing away money the day she graduated from high school, finally saving enough to get on a bus. She was twenty years old and had never been out of her area for more than a day. Sophie did not care how long she was gone or what happened next. She was doing what she wanted at last.

Sophie gazed left out her window at the unfamiliar landscape and wondered at this scenery: she was used to seeing flat farmland boxed in by the lines of trees that were field windbreakers—property delineated by fences. The rolling hills and meandering patches of trees she saw out her window now reminded her of her current situation: free from the bonds of northern Ohio's neatness.

Sophie reached up to touch her cheeks, shocked to find wetness. *Why am I crying?*

"Are you all right?" the man to her immediate right asked.

She turned to study her seatmate and wondered how she'd failed to note his presence. She'd been asleep when he sat down and lost in her thoughts since she woke. His scarred face and wild brown hair could have been frightening if not contrasted by gentle blue eyes rounded slightly by what looked like genuine concern. *He would be handsome if not for those horrible scars*, she thought, then felt guilty for her thoughts.

"I'm fine," she whispered. She sat up straighter and gave him what she hoped was a reassuring smile. "Really."

"Are you running away?" he asked, shocking her with his frankness.

"Yes," she answered. She wondered why she'd been honest. Probably because she didn't really have a reason not to be. She'd done nothing illegal, and he certainly didn't look like a police officer. He was probably just curious or thought she was younger than she was.

If he could be blunt and nosey, why couldn't she?

"Are those burn scars on your face?" she asked.

His expression reflected no insult. Instead, he smiled and answered: "It seems we're both good guessers." The remark made her laugh and relax against her seat.

"Husband trouble?" he asked next. She sighed deeply and looked back out her window.

"More like brothers and father and too-much-testosterone troubles."

It was his turn to laugh, and the deep-toned, musical sound surrounded her and somehow soothed her nerves.

"Big families can be a challenge, can't they?" he said when his laughter abated. The words drew her eyes back to his face.

As if he could feel her studying the scars, he said, "The barn caught fire when I was nine. I tried to save the horses, but I was too young to know what to do."

Sophie didn't even know what to say to that. His explanation meant he'd had to contend with disfigurement all his adult life. Yet he was accepting enough of his looks not to take offense at her abrupt question.

They were quiet for a few miles, each lost in thought. His next question broke the silence.

"How far are you going?" he asked, as if it was time for lighter conversation.

"As far as a $152 bus ticket would get me. I think my stub says Fredericksburg."

He smiled again, and the warmth of that smile erased the scars completely. He really did have an interesting face.

"Ah, a beautiful town. You'll love it. It's my hometown and I'm headed back. What are doing once you get there?"

"I'm finding a job…and hopefully an apartment. At least, that's the plan," she said.

"Sounds like a good plan," he said.

They relaxed back against their seats, staring straight ahead and letting the quiet of their individual thoughts rise up around them. Somehow the silence wasn't awkward.

"What kind of job will you look for?" he asked after a few minutes.

"I have no idea," she said. "I'm not really qualified for much. I can cook, and I can clean, but I have no desire to do either for a living. I only know the basics of computers. I've never been a waitress or a sales clerk. I don't have the strength or size for physical labor. But I know I'll find something."

She sensed him turn towards her, and when she looked his way, she saw a spark of excitement in his eyes.

"What about a receptionist position? You have a beautiful smile and your voice is pleasant. It's a job you learn as you go."

"Well that sounds good, but what made you think *receptionist*?"

He pulled at his lower lip as if letting his thoughts gel. "My brother is looking for someone to work at the front desk of his auto supply shop," he said. "It's a starter position, but he's a great guy to work for. I could introduce you."

Sophie felt the tears returning to her eyes but turned quickly away to hide them. Was this stranger sincere? His thoughtfulness touched her, but should it have frightened her as well? She rubbed away the tears and turned back to him.

"That sounds wonderful," she said. "But you don't even know me. And your brother. You don't think he'll consider me too inexperienced or even too small for a front desk job? I'm twenty but many people think I'm a child because my feet don't touch the ground."

"Oh … you consider yourself small?"

Really? she thought and glanced his way. She saw a teasing grin but didn't return the smile this time. Her size had caused her too much grief.

"Most people think I'm a dwarf or a midget, but I'm really just petite. Still, it makes it hard for people to take me seriously."

He continued to grin. "You're just perfection in a smaller package," he said.

She accepted his compliment by joining him in laughter, then they settled back into their seats again.

"Are you happy to be going home?" she asked. "Have you been away long?"

"Just a few days at a pharmacy convention," he said. "I own a small drug store in Fredericksburg. I could have taken a plane, but this is a pleasant ride and I avoid crowds … for obvious reasons."

She turned to study his profile. "Do your scars bother you?" she asked.

"Of course, but I've gotten used to it. Staring people are a fact of life. I actually find it refreshing when, instead of *wondering*, people like you just ask me what happened."

"I'm glad because I thought it was pretty rude of me," she said.

His illuminating smile returned.

"It's nice to talk to someone frankly, isn't it? To be this open," he said. His right hand came up and crossed his body to offer her a handshake. "David Franklin, at your service." She took the hand and squeezed it gently.

"Sophie Blackwell. A pleasure to meet you."

With that comment they both sat back again and closed their eyes, letting the rocking motion of the bus lull them into napping. An hour later, they were awakened by the sound of brakes and the intercom.

"Fredericksburg!" the driver announced.

They struggled into full wakefulness, gathered their possessions and got off the bus. In the parking lot, David turned to her. "Want to share a cab?" he asked. "I'm headed to the downtown area."

"That would be nice," Sophie said. "But I don't know exactly where I'm going. Leaving was … kind of an impulse; I made no reservations. Could you recommend a hotel?"

"I can," he answered. "The Sleep Inn is locally owned, but well run, clean and affordable. It's not too far from my brother's shop. We could stop there first if you'd like to talk to him about the job."

"Why not?" Sophie shrugged her shoulders. She couldn't believe how impulsive she was. She couldn't believe how much she trusted this stranger.

He hailed a cab and opened the back door inviting her to get in before him. When he was seated, he leaned over and gave an address to the taxi driver.

David's brother John was almost as friendly as David, though he seemed to be wound much tighter and his words were crisp and short, as if he was distracted. Within a few minutes of talking to him, Sophie found out why: his long-time receptionist had left the shop suddenly at a time when John was dealing with a bedridden pregnant wife who was having complications. He'd been balancing running the three-mechanic shop with being at home for her.

Sophie mostly listened while he explained his situation and what the job entailed. After twenty minutes of talking and only a few questions directed her way, he stood and said that if a background check revealed nothing amiss, and she could start right away, he was willing to give her a chance.

She couldn't believe her luck. She knew her family would think she was naïve, taking a cab with an unknown man, taking a job on a promise of payment, and she hesitated when David offered to carry her bag not only to the hotel but up to her room. But he left it at her hotel room door, promising to check on her the next day and suggesting places to look for an apartment.

After he left, Sophie sat on the bed in a daze. Without David's gentle eyes and reassuring presence, she was suddenly shaky. What had she done, getting on a bus by herself and just *leaving*? She didn't even know where to go for a meal. She lay down on the bed and turned to the wall. Ten minutes later, she turned back toward the ceiling. *This is ridiculous. I'm a grown woman.*

She hopped out of bed, consulted the front desk and left to buy a few items at a convenience store.

True to his word, David arrived the next morning at ten, newspaper in hand, several nearby apartments circled. It took most of a day and much walking, but before the supper hour, she'd found a place to live five blocks from her new job. It was small—one large room with a Murphy bed and galley kitchen—and was on the third floor of an older home. However, it was clean and cozy, furnished with well-worn, but comfortable tables and chairs, and it even had a window she could open to watch the foot traffic on the street. Best of all, she had enough money left from her bus trip to put down the deposit and first month's rent. She moved in the next day.

The next month of Sophie's life was challenging but rewarding. She fell into place at John's shop, learning how to schedule and run the front desk at a pace that allowed her, after only a few weeks, to take over when his wife finally had her baby.

For the first time in her life, Sophie was her own person—not her father's daughter, her brothers' keeper or "little one," the nickname she hated because it summed how her relatives saw her. She had her own job, a place to live, and best of all, a new friend. David kept in touch by text and phone and came to collect her once a week for a meal or a movie, whatever she felt she could afford. He didn't insist on paying or choosing the restaurant or movie. He didn't try to kiss or touch her in any way. He simply talked—about his life, about the town, about the world. Sometimes she wished he saw her as more than a friend, but for now, she was happy to have his companionship.

On her fifth week of freedom, hell knocked at her door, then stomped into her apartment in the form of Nick, her oldest brother, and his younger siblings Joseph and Jacob. How had they found her? She supposed it wasn't that hard; she'd used her real name and identification. She wasn't hiding from anyone, but she thought she'd have more time before her name popped up.

Into her orderly little place marched her brothers. Nick walked up to the visiting David and grabbed his shirt, pulling him almost nose to nose. The effect would have been comical since David was six inches taller and much stockier, except that Joseph and Jacob were at his side in seconds, poking David with their fingers as if he were a side of beef.

"Stop it right now, all of you," Sophie said.

They ignored her. "Is this the reason you left home?" Nick demanded. "This twerp get you pregnant?"

"No, you idiot. Let him go. I didn't even know him when I left. David is my new friend."

All three brothers' heads snapped around to gape at Sophie.

"I left because of you, you dolts. *All of you*. Now let him go."

Her words sunk in, and Nick dropped his hold and pushed, startling David and sending him backward to the floor. Sophie rushed to his side, running a hand over his head, smoothing back the curls on his forehead.

David smiled weakly and said, "I'm really not much of a fighter."

She leaned over and kissed him lightly on his cheek, then turned to glare up at her brothers, who now looked confused and, after a few moments under Sophie's burning eyes, embarrassed.

Nick found his voice first. "What do you mean you left because of us?"

Sophie rose to her feet, put her hands on her hips and faced all three of David's tormentors.

"I left home because you wouldn't let me do *any*thing. You used the excuse of protecting me, and I know you think it was out of love. But you should have realized I needed my own life. My own home. Look what you just did. David is just a friend, but you reacted in your usual manner – jumped to the conclusion he's a danger to me."

The brothers glanced at each other, then back at Sophie. They weren't used to their little sister's anger.

David pushed up off the ground, brushed off his jeans and straightened his shirt. He turned to address the brothers.

"I am just a friend, but you should know, I might want to be more than that at some point. Do you have a problem with that?"

His words reached toward Sophie and tugged at her heart. Their eyes connected, and he held her gaze. "I deliberately stayed in friend mode because I could see you needed space for now. I intended to ask you soon how you felt about this ugly mug of mine."

"Sophie needs someone to look after her. She's fragile and you're … *huge*," Joseph interjected.

David's eyes didn't leave Sophie's face. "She may have a small frame, but she's a giant inside."

"We don't want her hurt. It's our job to take care of her. She needs to be home," Jacob insisted.

"She *is* home," David said. He reached out and touched her cheek with his palm. His touch created a warmth at the center of her body that spread to all her extremities and settled in her heart.

Sophie broke the connection and turned from David to her brothers. They were galoots, but she knew they truly did love her. They'd had to be her "mother" because the only other woman in their lives had passed away from cancer when they were too young. She knew they blamed themselves for not being able to stop the disease or help their own mom. Her death had been the beginning of their excessive need to keep her safe. She knew it would be slow, but they would accept her decision to leave if she helped them.

"What you have to learn, Brothers, is that love sometimes means letting go. It's what every mother and father eventually has to realize so their baby can walk on its own," she said.

    She went to hug her family.

Adventures with Heroes

Genilee Swope Parente

At least we're not stranded in the middle of the desert, I thought to myself, looking around at the expansive green fields. A few miles back, the convertible midget BMW we were driving belched loudly, gurgled along for a few more minutes, then died with a dramatic sigh. Here we were on this lonely stretch of road, standing on a turnabout, staring at a plume of smoke drifting upward from the car's engine.

Sarah had borrowed the sporty, ancient car as an enticement to get me to come along on this trip—it had worked. We'd had a great adventure—our hair whipping in the wind, our voices singing loud and off-key to the radio. But as frequently happened with our adventures, we'd run into unforeseen troubles. We'd exited the boring strip of Highway 5 that ran through the desert to take a scenic back road and ended up here along the road without wheels that functioned.

I took in the rural landscape that surrounded us. Only one building was within sight, and I was pretty sure it was just a storage shed for a farmer. The most prominent features of this area were windmills; gentle giant sentinels of the fields, their sweeping arms reaching towards the vivid blue sky. They were an awesome site, but slightly scary to a girl used to neat suburban streets and pavement.

"What now?" I said, gazing back at my friend.

Sarah opened the hood, then bent low, coughing as she breathed in smoke. The cough turned into chuckles as her head popped back up.

"Why do we always lift the hood? I have *no* idea what I'm looking at here?"

As usual, her laughter pulled me in, and I giggled. The giggle turned into a scowl as I took out my cell phone to call Triple A. I was getting no signal in this part of California. I kicked the blacktop in frustration, then looked up to see waves of heat rising from the road ahead of us, a road that seemed to stretch towards infinity. "What the hell are we gonna do?"

"Brooooooooooooooooooooooooooooon. Broon." The sound came from behind me, then flew by on the road at my side, along with a long flash of grey. I now gazed at the back end of a huge semi truck chewing up the highway ahead of us.

"Son of a bitch! Why is he just honking at us! Driving by at sixty miles an hour, and he thinks we're going to be impressed with his big bad truck," I yelled at the quickly disappearing vehicle. I flipped him the bird knowing full well he was already too far ahead to see.

"Oh dear, he didn't even slow down to see what was going on," Sarah said. I heard the first glimmer of doubt about our situation in her tone. The long day driving and our current dilemma were finally getting to my usually brave friend.

Before I could catch myself, I started to think out loud: "Yea. If there aren't any houses and the drivers are crazy and don't bother to stop, and we can't get a signal …"

As quickly as I allowed my frustration to bubble to the surface, I pushed it back down. Negativity would do us no good. As always with Sarah and I, when one friend's silver lining started to tarnish, the other needed to take charge and hunt for the humor in the situation.

I coughed loudly, drawing her eyes toward me as intended. Lowering my voice and giving it an ominous tone, I whispered: "We have just escaped the clutches of the famous Highway Seven semi killer. He drives along back roads searching for his next victim. Fortunately for these damsels in distress, he just couldn't stop in time."

My story worked. Sarah smiled and added. "Meanwhile, coming down the road toward our two lovely ladies is the limo of a handsome, lonely millionaire. Our hero will spot two beautiful strangers standing on the side of the road and take pity on them. He'll offer champagne and his charm to soothe their frazzled nerves."

Our rescuer, however, did not turn out to be a limo owner with flutes. It was another semi truck, traveling much slower than the last. We saw it approach, heard the crunch of gravel as it pulled into the turnoff, then the grinding of gears as it rolled to a stop.

The passenger door of the giant cab creaked open and a heavily tattooed arm appeared followed by a giant head of thick grey and black hair. Between the heavy beard and a bushy mustache came the words: "Get in. My buddy says you need help."

I gaped at Sarah. Sarah gaped back at me, then raised her eyebrows. We both turned our heads to study our hero, who was dressed in wrinkly worn jeans and a denim jacket with the sleeves ripped off. The kerchief on his head failed in its attempt to keep his bounty of curly pepper and salt hair tied down.

"He cee-beed me, Gals. Said ya musta broke down. . ."

It dawned on Sarah and I at the same time what had happened: The trucker who had gone by first and honked had radioed his friend behind him to tell him we were stranded. While this did not mean it was wise to get into a truck with a total stranger, we agreed with a silent eye to eye nod to risk it: it was only the second vehicle we'd seen in the forty-five minutes we'd been on this road. What choice did we have? We didn't even know exactly where we were, and we didn't have a functioning cell phone. Besides, there were two of us and I knew we'd fight to the death to protect each other, though I wasn't sure what good that would do against a man who looked like he weighed more than both of us put together.

We got into his truck.

"Hey, thanks mister, that's really nice of you, if you could just let us use your cell or drop us off at the next town …," Sarah began.

"Or even get us someplace we could get a signal …," I continued. The guy glanced over at us, his eyebrows drawn together as if he didn't know what type of signal we meant.

I cleared my throat and began again.

"I'm Merilee and this is my friend Sarah. We were on way home and the car just died on us. I can't seem to get cell phone reception."

He harrumphed and said only one word: "Fred." His eyes returned to the road.

Okaaaaaay, I thought. Fred must be his name.

"Uh, about using your cell phone …," Sarah began, only to be interrupted by a crackling and a cheery voice.

"Breaker one nine. This is the red bird. Did you get the fillies OK, buddy?"

Fillies? Red bird?

Our host picked up a microphone, clicked a button and said, "Package pick up successful good buddy. We should get to the mill in about forty or so."

Package? Mill? I could feel Sarah squirm beside me.

"Well, buddy, we got us a slight 'nuther problem," the CB squawked back in the same cheerful tone.

"What be that, buddy boy?" our driver replied.

"I'm gonna run out a gas 'fore we get there."

Fred shook his head back and forth slowly, grumbling something too low for either of us to hear, then looked straight at us and emitted his first full sentence.

"That's Ricky fer ya. Man, I'm gonna kill that dude. He wouldn't remember his damn head if it weren't sittin' on his own neck. But his job is on the line if he runs out a gas," he muttered. The time it took for him to relay this information towards us allowed me a glimpse of deep honey-brown eyes and a mouth full of astoundingly white teeth. Neither fit the biker/trucker/tattoo image at all.

Turning his head back to the road he spoke into his mike: "Stop and I'll assist, man. Mile marker 54 there's another turnabout. We'll fix ya up."

Five minutes and several failed attempts at conversation later, Fred pointed to the passenger side door and made a circular motion to indicate Sarah should roll down her window. During this five minutes, he had spit forth four more phrases as answers to our attempts at chatting him up. He said: "Hate the things. Lindseyville. Sugar beets. 'Bout 4." The questions we'd asked were: "So do you have a cell phone?"

"Where are you headed?" "What are you hauling?" and "When will we get there?"

When the truck rolled to a stop at the turnabout, he added, "Only be a few. Shouldn't get too warm in here with the window open."

With that, he got out of his door and approached the truck he'd pulled up ahead of on the shoulder. We could see in the giant rearview mirrors mounted outside the windows that Ricky and Fred had their heads together conversing. Fred came back to the truck, foraged in the seat behind us and pulled out a rubber hose and what looked like a gasoline can, then returned to his friend. I turned to Sarah.

"Geez. They're siphoning gas. Do you really think a truck driver would run out of gas? Do you really think a truck driver would still use a CB and *not* have a cell phone?"

Sarah's eyes rounded, and I could tell her mind was grinding. She narrowed her eyes and assumed *her* best story-telling voice.

"The truck gang leaders search the back roads for women with car trouble or hitchhiking, stopping supposedly to help them. They are now deciding who will disable us by injecting us with drugs, who will carry the 'packages' to their destination: the human trafficking marketplace…"

While I appreciated her attempt to lighten the mood, it was a little too convincing. I pulled out my phone to check for a signal, then discovered the latest problem: the phone's battery was dead.

"Oh, God, this is like something out of the Twilight Zone," I whispered.

"Top of the afternoon to you two lovely ladies," a voice bellowed, making us jump. We looked toward the driver's side window where the voice was coming from, but couldn't see who was speaking.

Both of us leaned left over the giant steering wheel to peer out at a guy younger and much smaller than Fred with neatly trimmed carrot-colored hair, no beard, but the same bushy mustache. His jacket had sleeves, but they were rolled up to show off his forearm tattoos. A cigarette dangled from his lips. He jumped up on the sideboard and leaned slightly into the window. We backed away.

"My name's Richard, but my friends call me Ricky on account of my best friend's name is Fred, here, and we are like

Ricky Ricardo and Fred Mertz, you know what I mean? 'Cept I got the red hair instead of the wife. Saw you two was having some troubles back there, and well, I can't pass up the chance to be a knight in shiny armor …"

No problem with this one talking, I said to myself.

"… when the sitchey-ation calls for it. Course can't say as I've ever picked up anyone on this stretch of road. Not too traveled, 'cept those going to the mill. We should be there ourselves 'fore long. I don't got my cell with me or I'd let ya use it. Forgot the dang thing again, but Cilene has it with her. After we deliver these here beets to the mill, we'll take you by the hotel and you can call for help from the room. We never feel like making that haul back on the same day so we always meet up with the gals in the same place 'n go out to celebrate a run."

He seemed to realize he was throwing way too much information at us at once and abruptly shut his mouth.

"Uh, well, it might be better …," I began, but Ricky didn't give me a chance to finish. He pulled his small frame back from the cab's door, jumped down from the sideboard and was replaced by Fred, who opened the door, nodded at his friend, then jumped into the cab and put us back on the road.

Sarah and I gave up the idea of conversation then and sat silently, wondering how we'd get out of going to a hotel with two strange men.

Two events during the next ten minutes convinced us we were probably not going to die from these two truckers' hands.

"Breaker one nine. This is Candy Cane Sweetheart. Wonderin' where you are, honeybunch."

"Scuse me, ladies," Fred said politely as he reached for the microphone again.

I didn't really follow all of what the two said back and forth though I gathered Candy was Fred's girl or wife, and she and the aforementioned Cilene would be waiting at the hotel. What hit me more than the words was Fred's face as he talked. I glanced in his driver's rearview mirror, and though it was difficult to see much skin beneath all that hair, the tough-guy image melted quickly when I studied his eyes. Sarah and I and this truck no longer existed for this man—only the woman whose voice came through. I sought out Sarah's face, knowing she would be watching him as well and silently mouthed the words: this guy is in love. Sarah gave another slight nod.

The second event happened once we pulled up into the mill area, which looked like a giant version of the game Chutes and Ladders—conveyer belts and tall straight walls around giant towers. About a dozen other trucks were in the lot awaiting their turn to rid their truck beds of beets. Fred and Ricky were greeted warmly by at least half a dozen other drivers, who glanced our way shyly but didn't approach us, except for one guy who came over to our truck long enough to hand Sarah a cell phone. Sarah called her boyfriend and arranged for him to pick us up at the Hotel 9 where our rescuers were staying.

Leaving behind the two loads of beets, our rescuers' trucks traveled the short distance to the motel, parking behind the long square building in a giant lot where a few other trucks rested. Ricky picked up keys in the lobby, and we were soon within the confines of a room with orange and brown curtains and bedspreads that looked like they might disintegrate with one touch. The room's drabness was warmed up, however, by a smattering of feminine accouterments—a tube of mascara resting on the television, a blouse hanging from a chair, several round brushes on the nightstand. The scent in the room was a mixture of powder and flowers.

Fred took in the smell ever so slightly, then groused about the sloppiness. He proceeded to empty his pockets of loose change and dollar bills, adding to the mess. Ricky walked in behind Sarah and plopped on a bed with a tired sigh. Sarah and I stood awkwardly not knowing quite what to do with ourselves since there was only one chair in the room.

We were saved from deciding by the loud arrival of Fred's and Ricky's female companions. They burst through the door carrying plastic grocery bags and squealed when they realized their men were there. One was tall with platinum blond hair and an abundance of breast and tattooed arms while the other was small and wiry with short spiky black hair and muscled arms peeking out from pink puffy sleeves. They noticed us standing there, and I had to stop myself from cringing. The women looked like they'd have no trouble trouncing two female "rivals."

The short one tilted her head, then cracked a huge smile, completely disintegrating any aura of danger.

"Well, hi, honeys. You must be the two gals our boys done rescued."

She introduced herself as Candy, and I couldn't help thinking her name matched her disposition—sweet.

"We bought some wine, and I know you could use a bit right 'bout now," she said as she set the bags down and took out a large box.

The other woman, who had to be Cilene, went into the bathroom and came back out with two plastic cups. She was taller than her Ricky and looked like she could pound him if she wanted to, but she smiled as warmly as Candy and filled the cups with pale pink liquid from the box. She offered the drinks to Sarah and me with a shy smile. We accepted with dazed "thanks," and she turned back to address the men.

"Not to be rude to these here gals, but we gotta go, boys," Cilene said. "We promised Boz and Betty we'd meet 'em at the Circle Heart at seven, and it's already that now. You know the line gets really long. Let's leave these gals here in the room where they'll be safe to wait for their friend and scoot our booties."

With much shaking of hands, a few more attempted "thanks" from both me and Sarah and a mumbled "s'all right" from Fred, our rescuers and their ladies were suddenly gone.

Their departure somehow felt like the end of this installment of The Adventures with Sarah and Merilee. The room felt too quiet. We looked at each other, downed the sickeningly sweet wine in one gulp and plopped our rears on the beds across from each other. Then we burst into laughter. As the laughter slowly trickled away, I glanced around the room, ready to launch into the recap and analysis of what had just happened to us, but what I saw stopped me.

On the table were wads of dollar bills. Over the chair, one of the ladies had left her purse. On the nightstand was a cell, probably Ricky's forgotten phone. On the desk were a set of keys, a small PC and what I took to be some kind of portable CB. They'd left all their personal belongings behind without a thought about who *we* might be.

My eyes came around to Sarah's, and I could see she was thinking along the same lines. These people, who had just met us, jumped in to help, then trusted the situation and their own instincts enough to leave us here with their stuff.

I swiped my mouth with one hand, then dropped it into my lap.

"Sarah, my dear. I'm afraid we can't call ourselves the heroes or the heroines of this particular story. The heroes just left to dine at the great Circle Heart."

The Gift Box

F. Sharon Swope

Benjamin wedged his body into the space under the rock ledge. He'd been here many times before—it was his thinking place, his great escape, a place he was pretty sure no one else visited regularly. He'd never seen other footprints in the sand leading up to here.

Benjamin first found this spot when he was just ten, a boy who was small for his age. To him, this giant, under-a-rock-ledge space was a place of adventure, but also somewhere to hide. It wasn't a cave, it was too shallow and not underground. However, when he was a boy, a rounded-out hole worn into the far wall of the space was large enough for him to sit in without anyone seeing him—even those who might be walking along the water's edge. The ledge above his head kept him cool on a hot day and helped to hide the cut-out spot where he usually sat.

He is here today trying to deal with turning age fifty-one, but so far it hasn't worked. It just reminds him he's been coming to this spot for more than forty years to dream his dreams, plan his plans. And in that time—what has he really accomplished? None of his dreams or goals have been reached.

Certainly not those he had at ten when he dreamed of finding a pirate's treasure hidden under the sand. He planned to dig that chest up, sell the gold and jewels and give the money to his mother. Maybe then, she would look at him with admiration instead of disdain.

By the time Benjamin was fourteen, he'd stopped thinking about treasure but not about gaining his mother's respect. He came to this spot as a teen to plot out his life. He would work hard and become a doctor—maybe a plastic surgeon who would earn gobs of money while also fixing his own looks. He was sick of everyone calling him "Dumbo" because of his ears or "Durante" because of his nose. It was a constant joke at his school, and he laughed right along with his fellow students. They never saw his tears. He always came here to do his crying.

By the time he turned sixteen, he'd given that dream up as well, helped along by a mom who constantly called him dense and teachers who reminded him he wasn't an achiever. *"If you can't even pass science, how do you expect to get into medical school?"*

When Benjamin's mother died during his junior year of high school, he gave up the idea of going to college as well. There was no money, and he became a ward of the state until he could reach age eighteen, passing through several foster homes and, ironically, ending up back at his own school as a janitor when he struck out on his own. The big nose and dumbo ears remained, an excuse he gave himself for never meeting his dream girl.

So here he was under this rock, more than half his life gone, still single, still awkward and still coming back to this spot. Benjamin sighed and laid back on the sand; he no longer fit into the cutout on the wall. Yet he still found comfort from this spot. The waves had a hypnotic effect: in and out, in and out, not quite reaching the spot where he lay. What would happen if they did? What would it feel like to let the water reach out with its magical fingers to encircle him and pull him out to sea? Would he never worry about things again?

He closed his eyes and was almost asleep when he heard the splash. Benjamin almost hit his head sitting up, remembering just in time he was too close to the underbelly of the ledge.

Was that a box floating on the water?

The box sunk into the valley of a wave, then rose again on the crest of the next one, coming closer to the shore. Benjamin wiggled his body out from under the rock, then stood and climbed over the stones to reach the water's edge. He heard a mewl and thought: "Someone is drowning a litter of kittens."

He waded into the water far enough to reach the box and encircle it with his arms to tug it back to shore. The mewing got louder. He searched for a way to open the box and found a grip on the strong tape at the top. When he had it off, he slowly opened the flaps, hoping the kittens wouldn't escape before he could help them.

Instead of finding kittens, however, he found a baby. It was wrapped in a towel and whimpering softly, and when Benjamin bent to pick it up, he felt violent shivers from the bundle he held. Who had thrown a baby into the freezing water? What should he do? The first thing had to be getting the baby warm.

Benjamin unzipped his jacket and cradled the infant to his chest, then zipped the jacket back up so the small body would not fall out. Without really thinking it through, he raced to his car and started it, turning up the heater. Once behind the wheel, he wondered where to go. Should he drive straight to the hospital? An emergency care center? The police?

Instead of heading to any of them, however, he drove the few blocks to his home, driven by the instinct that the top priority was a safe and warm place. He couldn't believe someone had thrown a child in the water. Had they been trying to get rid of their own kid?

Inside his house, he unzipped his coat and laid the baby on his couch. Miraculously, the infant had not gotten very wet; the water hadn't had enough of a chance to seep through. The little one was dressed in a sleeper whose little pink lambs indicated he'd probably rescued a girl. She looked at him with rounded eyes the color of the water where she'd been thrown, not making more than the whimpering sound but continuing to quake. He wedged her in with a couch pillow and went to find some blankets, then wrapped her and rocked her until she seemed to settle and stop shivering.

Then he peeled back the top of the blanket and gazed into her face. Her tiny nose was no bigger than the button on his shirt; her lips puckered then puffed out like a blossoming flower. Her eyelashes were long and whispery against her cheek, and she had a thin layer of brown fuzz on her head. He saw now that the sea blue of her eyes also contained a few tiny flecks of sandy brown. Those eyes stared up at him with a calm, curious expression as if to say: And who might you be?

Then her face crumpled and erupted into distress, her cries filling the empty corners of his apartment.

Oh god, oh god. What to do, he thought. He had very little experience with babies. Benjamin stood and began to pace, putting the baby on his shoulder as he'd seen other people do with their children and patting her back. *She's probably hungry,* he thought. She needed a bottle or squished up food or … what did babies at that age eat?

And how old *was* this child? She didn't look like a newborn, but she barely weighed anything.

A picture formed in his head of the lady who lived next door. He didn't really know her except to exchange polite hellos at the mailbox, but he remembered watching as another woman dropped a little toddler off at her door. He'd assumed that the lady—*Agnes, Agnes was her name. Agnes Foster.* He'd assumed that Agnes Foster was a babysitter. She'd know what to do with a baby.

Benjamin stood at Agnes' door, the howling baby's screams now flooding the hall. He was just about to knock when the door flew open.

"Goodness. What is that racket?"

At the sound of the woman's exclamation, the baby quieted, and

Benjamin took her off his shoulder and into his cradled arms. Was that curiosity etched on her tiny face? Surely she was too young for such a reaction. The baby twisted her head towards Agnes's voice.

"Oh, how adorable. Is she your grandbaby?" Agnes's usually stiff posture seemed to transform. Her spine relaxed and a huge smile erupted on her face. Even the woman's voice changed, rising in baby sing-song.

"What'sa matter little darlin' Why are you crying outside my door?" She looked at Benjamin and asked, "Is there something the matter? Is your baby sick?"

Benjamin had to think fast. He didn't really want to explain how he'd come to be holding a baby outside this woman's door—he just needed her help.

"Mrs. Foster is it? Hi. I'm Benjamin Goodman your neighbor?"

"Yes, I recognized you."

"Ah, my daughter left … Millie … with me and forgot to leave her diaper bag. I didn't realize it until Millie here started to cry. I was just wondering …"

Agnes chuckled, and Benjamin breathed a sigh of relief. The lie had rolled so easily off his tongue.

"Your daughter must be a new mother. Her mind is still addled from nine months of slavery to this one," she said. "She'll be back at your door within the hour, I guarantee. In the meantime, come on in. I have supplies at my house for my own grandbaby Ronnie."

By this time, she'd swung open the door and was retreating back into her apartment. Benjamin followed.

In her kitchen, Agnes motioned to the table and pulled out a chair. Benjamin continued to stand, the baby at his shoulder again. She was making gurgling sounds and swiveling her head as if trying to get a glimpse of her surroundings.

Agnes stood at the frig, the light from inside the door reflected on her face. It struck Benjamin that she was probably about his age, *but a whole lot better looking*. Why had he never noticed that?

"It's probably fine to give Millie a bit of Ronnie's formula, or does her mom breastfeed exclusively?" She stood with one hand on the frig door, her eyebrows raised in question.

Breastfeed? He had no idea what to say. The image of a baby at a woman's breast embarrassed him. But wasn't it the norm to go natural these days?

"Uh, yea, of course. I mean: yes she's breastfed. But I know my daughter gives Millie milk in between times."

"Formula, you mean," Agnes said, reaching into the frig. "Yes, Sally, my daughter has trouble expressing her milk. She's started Ronnie on formula for half his feedings and says he seems more satisfied."

Benjamin didn't even want to know what expressing was.

Agnes leaned into the frig, took out a plastic bottle and popped it into the microwave, then set the timer. Meanwhile, "Millie" had started wailing again and Benjamin began to bounce her gently on his shoulder as he stood, not really knowing why he was doing it.

"You're good with her," Agnes said. The timer went off and she took the bottle out and squirted some of its contents onto her wrist.

"What do you mean *good* … she's bawling her eyes out!" Benjamin pointed out.

Agnes chuckled again. "Yes, she's hungry. I meant that you've got the grandpa shuffle down. She knows food's coming. She's already quieting."

Agnes was right. The cries had lessened. For some reason, that made Benjamin feel good—almost proud. *Would he have been a good daddy?*

"Do you mind if I feed her?" Agnes asked.

Since Benjamin had no idea how to get the baby to actually eat, he felt a profound sense of gratitude this woman had volunteered. He handed over little "Millie."

Agnes settled Millie on her lap, the tiny head cradled on one arm, her other hand holding the bottle. She brushed the nipple against the baby's lips until Millie found what she needed and latched on.

"So how old? I'm guessing only a few weeks or maybe two months?"

"Uh, yea. That's right. A month," Benjamin said, glad Agnes was taking the lead on conversation. He needed time to think. *What was he going to do? If he told her the truth, she'd probably call the cops. Maybe that was for the best. They could find the baby's parents. But they might think he'd stolen her. And what if it was her very own parents who'd dumped her into the ocean?*

"Did she have a difficult birth?" Agnes asked.

"Well, no, I think Millie was fine throughout the process," Benjamin replied, then was startled when Agnes threw back her head and practically guffawed.

"I'm sure she *was*. Millie had been waiting nine months to get into the world. But I meant your daughter. Was she in labor long?"

Oh lord, what was long?

"Um, I wasn't actually there." *At least that much was true.* But why was he lying about this?

"I understand. No need for grandpa at the delivery I suppose. I'm sure her husband took good care of her." Agnes's entire attention was focused on the baby, who was busy sucking gently, her eyes starting to flutter closed between sips.

Agnes's comment made Benjamin wonder: was there a father? Did he abandon a desperate woman? But even if that happened, how could anyone—male or female—throw a baby off a rocky ledge? If he did go to the cops, would they eventually return the child to whoever did this?

Thankfully, Agnes' questions about labor and breastfeeding and his supposed daughter gave way to a constant steady chattering about her grandson Ronnie—when he first rolled over and what words he seemed to be trying to say. She apparently watched the boy several times a week while her daughter went back to work part-time.

Benjamin stopped really listening, drawn to the baby's gentle sucking and sweet face. Her eyelids were mostly closed now as she took in needed nourishment and succumbed to the lure of comfort. Agnes laid down the bottle and put the baby to her shoulder to pat gently until she heard the desired burp.

"Well, I'm pretty sure you now will have a sleeping granddaughter for a while," Agnes said, standing and holding the baby out to Benjamin. She then reached into the frig for a second bottle and extracted a diaper from the bag by the couch. "Better take these just in case it takes your daughter a while to realize she forgot to leave her supplies."

"Thank you, Mrs. Foster. I really appreciate this ...," he mumbled awkwardly.

"Oh please. Call me Agnes," she said.

Back in the apartment, Benjamin sat in his favorite chair, the baby cradled in one of his blankets and sleeping in his arms. She was so beautiful. So tiny and perfect.

What should he do? He wondered for the first time if he could get away with just keeping her. Would anyone ever know if he did? After all, someone had simply discarded this child—thrown her into the water like so much garbage. Wasn't it fate that he was under that ledge just when the child needed rescuing? Was she some kind of miracle birthday gift from a higher being?

But if he kept her, what would that entail? Benjamin laid the snoozing baby gently back on the couch and pushed the pillows around her so she wouldn't move, then got up and went to his desk and computer. Surely Google could help him make a list of the supplies he'd need to keep a baby happy.

Formula, diapers, baby clothes, toys to stimulate her mind, burping clothes, baby blankets, baby bath, special soap for the baby's skin…. He wrote it all down on a notepad.

The list grew and grew, but Benjamin didn't care. He had very little to spend money on these days and his savings account reflected that reality.

Benjamin then switched to articles on baby care and began to read. Lord, it was a task trying to keep a baby healthy. He read for almost an hour, then sat back and stretched his shoulders. *Could he really pull this off? Maybe he could befriend Agnes some more and come up with a story about his daughter dying and how he was stepping in to raise the baby.*

Yes, that made sense. He would make friends with Agnes, maybe even get her to do things together with their grandbabies.

The baby was making gurgling sounds again. Benjamin looked over at the couch and rose to go to her, then sat down abruptly. He needed to do one more thing. Benjamin went back to google and typed in "recent kidnappings," "Savannah, Georgia," and there it was: "Baby Disappears Out of Home," and "Parents Heartbroken Over Kidnapping," and finally "No Word from Kidnappers Yet on Ransomed Baby."

It couldn't be. It just couldn't be. The baby was crying again and Benjamin went to her. He cradled and rocked her and sang softly, a tune he remembered from his youth, though he knew it couldn't have been his mother singing. It had to have been one of several nannies. His mother never cared enough to sing him a lullaby. It seemed to work with Millie, though. Her sobbing stopped at the same moment his tears began.

Benjamin looked at the ceiling and swore.

"How could you give me this gift, God. Then take her away in the same afternoon?"

He was fifty-one. His life had gone nowhere. He'd never even got his act together enough to have children. He was worthless.

His black thoughts were interrupted, however, by a touch. He blinked to clear up his tears then looked down to discover that somehow, the baby had managed to grasp his little finger. He wiggled the finger, but the baby didn't let go. She held on and Benjamin was amazed at how much strength a tiny baby could have. She didn't exactly smile at him—Benjamin was sure she was too young for that. But her eyes seemed to focus on his face for a second.

Benjamin smiled. The baby *had* been a gift from God. But he knew he had to reciprocate with a gift of his own—there were parents worried sick about this girl. He picked up the phone to call the police.

Different Seats

Genilee Swope Parente

Stephen Ward's snores drifted up from the tired-looking blue lounger that Betsy Ward hated to vacuum. She leaned forward to see beyond the wings of her chair and shuddered at the sight of that lounger. Whenever she tried to clean it, it threatened to fall apart—the fabric was worn through in a couple of places, stuffing had to be pushed back in, and the footrest needed a hard tug before it would release. Betsy wondered for the thousandth time why her husband fought so hard against her offer to replace it with a nice leather recliner. He'd grumbled about the waste of money and insisted his chair had done him just fine for all these years. He'd never recognized the aesthetic sacrifice she'd made by allowing that abomination to exist among her carefully selected, well-balanced mix of living room furniture.

Betsy sat back in her own chair and sighed. She dropped her knitting in her lap and rubbed her hands along the armrests. She knew he hated her chair almost as much as she hated his. The busy pattern of the fabric hurt his eyes, he said, and he couldn't understand how someone could sit in a wing-backed chair without getting a stiff back. Betsy was proud to own this expensive piece of furniture.

She liked how well her formal chair went with the pale blue couch where visitors sat, and she was willing to trade some comfort for beauty. She managed to keep it in prime condition by covering the seat with a scratchy shawl the cat hated. She also believed the stiffness of this chair made visitors forego sitting here, which meant the costly piece of furniture would last a long time. His ratty old thing would be around forever simply because he was stubborn and because most people who came to the Ward home averted their eyes completely from the worn lounger. They weren't about to sit in it.

Betsy supposed these two chairs were one of those things a couple who had been together for fifty-one years deserved to argue about—a means to let off a little steam once in a while over something that wasn't really important. They kept the few real fights they'd had during their marriage for the really big issues—children, money, jealousy when someone paid too much attention to one or the other spouse. Those topics had caused the few major battles they'd had over the years; doozies that ended in a night in the hotel for him and, in one case, a week shuffling between kids for her. Who *wouldn't* have fights when you live on a limited income but have raised four kids who were very different from each other—whose unique-to-that-personality problems occasionally pitted one parent against the other. They didn't do it on purpose, her kids, but it happened too often because Betsy and Stephen didn't always see eye to eye on how to get involved.

Betsy smiled and sat back against the flowered fabric. The children also had been the main source of celebration and togetherness for her family. Just last year, on their fiftieth anniversary, the kids had paid for a lavish cruise for their parents. She closed her eyes and remembered the blue of the water, the smell of sunscreen, the glitter of the boat's chandeliers and the elaborate meals. Even Stephen couldn't complain about a vacation where the crew existed to fulfill their every desire. The days were spent doing activities they weren't used to anymore: dancing, chatting with strangers, games of shuffleboard, nightly shows in the theater. Their bodies had balked at the unexpected exercise, but their muscles were soothed by the afternoon sunshine and a couple of massages for each of them. When Stephen had reached for her hand during one late-afternoon movie, she'd felt again the simple thrill of being on a date, something she hadn't felt in a long time.

Betsy picked up her knitting, thought about turning off the TV, then decided the background noise was a soothing accompaniment to the rhythm of her needles. When this year's anniversary came around, the kids hadn't even thought to call. But who could complain after such an elaborate gesture the year before? Stephen and Betsy had celebrated this year in their usual manner: a mostly silent steak dinner at Applebee's and a shared bottle of celebratory wine.

Betsy sighed and laid down her needles for a moment, letting her mind stretch further back. How had two people as different as her and her husband ever come to be a couple?

Betsy and Stephen had started out as coworkers at a small, twice-weekly newspaper. He was a photographer with a talent for seeing things through the viewfinder that no one else saw—the pictures he produced were far superior to any the town of Edonsville had ever seen. She was a reporter with a reputation for accuracy, as well as an acerbic manner that allowed her to get away with throwing tough questions at town officials despite the fact they came from a woman in the days when female opinions were not readily welcomed, much less accepted.

Stephen had worked in Edonsville only one year, swept up by a nearby city magazine that had tracked his talent for using the camera. She'd been sad to see him go—she hadn't had many friends on staff, and she knew she'd miss his teasing. The hole his absence created was far deeper than she expected. They stayed in touch, writing long letters that became ever-more complicated and visiting each other when one of them could scrape together the money for a train ride. It took almost five years for him to convince her she needed to take the leap and leave a job with minimal pay and too many hours. She'd moved to his city, taken a well-paid job that had nothing to do with journalism and everything to do with her organizing abilities, and finally agreed to date him.

The sound of gunfire interrupted her reflections and his snores. Jim Rockford of the Rockford files was caught up in yet another television plot in which bad guys were trying to kill him for interfering in their business.

"H-m-m. What time is it?" Stephen mumbled.

"It's only eight. You fell asleep during the opening credits," she replied.

The light was growing dim in the room, and both Betsy and Stephen reached for the lamp that sat between them. He won the race and pulled the cord.

Picking up the paper sprawled on his lap, he flipped to the back page.

"Weather's not getting better tomorrow."

"Em hmm," she said. The clicking of her needles resumed. "Don't forget we have a nine a.m. appointment to get our picture taken for the kids' Christmas gift. I've laid out your blue pants and light green shirt to wear," she said.

"I can pick out my own damn clothes," he grumbled. But the words held no animosity.

"You know you look good in those pants and that shirt. Wear the tie with light green and blue stripes."

The telephone rang and her clicking needles stopped. Betsy rose from her chair, rubbed her neck and walked the fifteen steps to the hallway, knowing there was plenty of time to answer. Their family and friends knew their phone was set to ring eight times before letting the machine pick up.

"We can't be there, Doris," Betsy said into the phone. "He has to take the car in on Friday and get it waxed and detailed before our road trip next week. I think that car wash is a waste of money, but you know how men are."

He looked up from his paper and swiveled to glare at her, but made no comment.

"That was Doris," Betsy said as she hung up.

"So it was," he said. His eyes had returned to the sports page.

"She invited us to lunch on Friday. I said we couldn't make it," she said.

"I know," he said. "I'm sitting right here."

"She agrees with me that the new place in town is a waste of money. Twenty-five dollars for a wash and wax when you know Jimmy would do it for just ten bucks," she said.

"Jimmy doesn't make it shine," he said. "He doesn't clean out the cup holders."

She sighed deeply, but returned to her chair and picked up her knitting. She supposed if they could afford her twice-a-month manicure, they could afford a cleaner car.

The television show ended and another began. The scarf she was knitting for the church bazaar got longer. At ten p.m., the clock on the stairway wall chimed. They'd bought that clock because its swinging cat tail made them laugh, and she'd been relieved to find just that right spot on the stairwell, a spot hidden from those on the couch. The clock was a little tacky in her view, but they'd grown accustomed to the sound of the swishing tail and the warning chimes. The clock's sound seemed to synchronize their sighs, bringing them both to their feet automatically. As they did almost every night, they carried their tired bones up the stairs to their room. Stephen brushed his teeth with an expensive natural toothpaste that featured a green leaf on its label. She hated the taste of it and always used her Colgate. *If you're going to save the planet, there are a thousand ways other than crummy toothpaste*, she thought for the hundredth time as he brushed.

They crawled into bed and lay on their backs looking at the wall of family pictures opposite their feet, something they did nearly every night.

"Sissy never should have married that bum; I'm glad his fat ass left," Stephen said. "Are we taking the kids this weekend?"

"He wasn't that fat, Stephen. But I agree he was an ass." They both chuckled. It was rare they brought up Sissy's bad marriage. It was rarer still that Betsy used the word, "ass."

Betsy yawned.

"Jonah and Amy are watching the kids again this weekend. I don't know what our Sissy would do without her brother and his sweet wife. I don't know how Amy finds time to help out. Course if they had their own kids. . .," But she could sense him turning away from her onto his side. Conversation for today had come to a halt. It was time for sleep. She rolled over in the same direction as he faced and scooted close so she could rest one hand on his back. They never stayed in that position long, but they began most nights this way.

A strange noise broke through the fog and the darkness, and Betsy lay for a moment coming into wakefulness. What had she been dreaming about?—something about keeping the cat safe in the midst of a gun battle. The noise sounded again and Betsy wondered if KittyKat was in distress. But the sound was coming from behind her. She flipped over to see Stephen laying on his back again, clutching his stomach. She threw back the covers, sprang to the floor and was at his side of the bed in seconds.

"What is it, Stephen? What hurts?"

"I don't know. My stomach. My side. Everything. Gas maybe. Just give it a minute."

She felt his forehead for fever, then realized how foolish that reaction was. This wasn't one of the kids coming down with the flu. The glow from the nightlight showed his face scrunched up, his breathing shallow and sharp in reaction to pain. She picked up the phone and dialed 911.

"No, really, I'm sure it will be all right in a minute or ... ehhhhhh. Aren't I too old to have babies?" he said.

Betsy filed away the joke as a good sign and rattled off the necessary information to the EMTs, never taking her eyes off his face. She was in automatic pilot mode, and she knew he wouldn't object—it was how they were in a crisis.

The EMTs arrived and a flurry of activity began. They took his vitals, called in the results by radio, eased him onto a rolling cart and were wheeling him out the door when one of them stopped to ask if she'd be riding in the ambulance or following in her car. She didn't even hesitate before answering, "car," even though she hadn't done much driving in recent years—to local card games, her ladies club, the salon—places he didn't go.

As she grabbed the keys and headed out the door, she remembered that the last two times the ambulance had been called, she'd been the one on the gurney, and he hadn't even thought before leaping into the vehicle.

This was different somehow. She needed that car to take him home because this could *not* be anything serious. She would not allow it. He had a healthy heart, and the pain wasn't coming from his chest anyway. He'd already had his appendix out so it wasn't about to rupture.

But as she drove into the night, watching the red lights ahead of her, she longed for the feel of his hand clutching hers and wondered if it would have been better to ride along. Why had she decided to drive? What's more, when and why had she *stopped* driving whenever the two were together? He'd never been a good passenger—nervous and fidgety and not sure what to do with himself. But why did men always feel the need for control, and why did women always think they had to create the illusion men *had* that control? Why did women give up the steering wheel or the remote without more of a fight?

Her hands were shaking, and she knew her brain was addled, but she got to the hospital safely, parked the car and went into overdrive. She demanded to know where he was and why she couldn't see him right there and then. Once she was in the tiny room where they'd placed him, finally holding his hand, she drilled the nurses about what the monitors meant, how soon the doctor would arrive, why the room was so cold, why they couldn't give him something for pain. She made sure the doctor knew that penicillin was not something his body could tolerate. She asked the orderlies for more pillows, more ice.

Betsy knew the emergency staff would label her difficult, but she didn't care. Her husband's lack of scolding for her rude behavior really had her worried. He lay flat on his back his face towards her as the medication that finally came after the doctor's evaluation and a few tests kicked in. He didn't say anything at all as she spewed forth stories he'd already heard a million times. He kept his eyes trained on her face.

"Anyway, when Uncle Benjamin got to the emergency room, his blood-alcohol level was something like point one five—it was a good thing he hadn't been driving. And this was after church! He insisted he hadn't touched a drop and those of us who know his teetotal-ing self couldn't believe this was happening. The doctors said he had something called gut fermentation syndrome. Can you imagine that? His big old belly was its own brewery."

She saw his lips twitch either in an attempt to smile or in reaction to pain.

"Then there was Kathy McGuire, my cousin Terry's friend. That girl was so huge, she didn't even know she was pregnant …"

Four hours later, Betsy sat in a hard plastic chair at his side, smoothing the too-few hairs back onto his forehead with her hand.

"You're going to be fine—just fine. The gallstones are gone. They decided to take your gallbladder, too, but they said it wasn't a big deal. Because of your age, they are keeping you overnight. I'm staying at Doris' house since it's so close, but I'll be back in the morning to get you."

He reached for her hand, squeezed his eyes shut tight again and groaned.

"You're feeling your stomach area hurt because the anesthesia is just wearing off now. The nurses will give you something. You won't feel a thing pretty soon."

"Tell that to my damn pain center," he said. "I don't think it's quite got the message."

She saw a small smile begin at the sides of his mouth. Just a tiny break in the clouds, but she knew the crisis was almost over.

She leaned over to tickle the center of his belly, avoiding the area with bandages.

"Hey pain center, go the hell. Leave my husband alone."

He looked at her then, and she saw in the depths of his gaze what he was seeing: the short, petite woman whose hair used to be so dark, it made his pulse quicken. A woman who, despite her small stature, was bossy, sometimes brassy and always ballsy. He squeezed her hand.

Betsy smiled for the first time in twelve hours and allowed the thought that had pinged at the exterior of her mind to finally form: what would life be like without him to challenge her and dig out the lighter side of her personality?

She abolished the question as quickly as it had come. *I was right to bring the car*, she thought. *We'll both be going home soon.*

Shedding Her Skin

F. Sharon Swope

My name is Charity Williams. It's a pretty name, and I've always liked it, but I never felt it matched who I am. It sounds like a character in a romance novel—the perky girl with bouncy blonde curls, a curvy and diminutive frame, and maybe a demure manner that makes boys want to protect her. The kind of girl who might be good at batting her lashes.

Instead, I look like a tree trunk. I'm tall, big boned and lacking in defined curves, though I've always had plenty of muscle. My hair is dull brown; my eyes are the color of baby poop, and boys are more intimidated than chivalrous around me. I'm not particularly creative or crafty, a lover of poetry, violins or even watercolor painting.

Oh, I'm smart and I have my interests in life, but those interests run along the lines of what men enjoy: sports, cars and numbers—I love numbers. More than one person has labeled me "gay" but I take no offense. It's simply not true; I like men.

I do have one redeeming quality in the eyes of most of the male population: I'm filthy rich.

This doesn't give me much joy because the money reflects one of the worst periods of my life. When I was just twenty, my parents won the lottery—seven million dollars. They decided to take a lump sum, went out and bought a brand new Maserati, then crashed that fancy piece of driving machinery into a tree on the way home from the dealership. That left me orphaned and living in a cocoon of grief that took me almost five years and many hours of therapy to escape.

When I finally broke out of my bubble of sorrow, I developed a skill that turned my parents' millions into many more dollars—I'd found a new friend: the stock market. Yet even back then I recognized I wasn't really living a full life.

A year ago Rick Mansfield walked into my life, bringing fun and good times and personal attention. He took me places I'd never been; showed me how other young people live today; encouraged me to reach out and find ways to make my uncomely self a more attractive package. Deep down, I knew Rick was probably only showering me with his time because of my wealth. But I didn't care. He was gorgeous and well-educated, and he knew how to make me feel human. His skill at charm and good looks were the reasons he was sought after by almost every single female in our town. Yet he also treated me with respect—I knew he admired my mind even if he did not admire my body. Why shouldn't I wake up next to him every day of my life and maybe make beautiful babies?

    I accepted his proposal of marriage and entered one of the most thrilling periods of my life: planning a grand wedding that every girl in town would envy. I had the money; I had the desire to do it right. I selected the most beautiful, expensive dress I could find, with tons of lace and real pearls sewn into the bodice. The train would need two attendants just to hold it up as I paraded past pretty women who I guessed would be green with envy. I ordered doves to be released at the end of the ceremony, the biggest cake from the most expensive bakery; shrimp cocktails, huge T-bones and lobsters for the wedding dinner. I spent two blissful months going a little crazy about everything, and I don't think I've ever had a better time.

    The day before my wedding it all came crashing down. The doubts that hadn't even fluttered their wings were suddenly flying about like a swarm of bees escaping from a disturbed hive. What was I doing? I didn't love Rick; I really didn't even *like* him that much. He was too cocky and full of himself, and I was pretty sure he'd eventually cheat. I certainly enjoyed looking at him, and I ate up the attention he provided. But I was about to commit myself to a life with him just for the sake of pretty babies.

I am not the type to go back on a promise, however; and really, what alternative was there? Would anyone else want to marry me? Besides, someone had to wear that gorgeous dress, release those doves, walk down that aisle. Why not me?

I put on my gown two hours before the ceremony, just to give me back my resolve and confidence. It didn't work.

As I walked down the aisle, I felt like I was wearing a $25 dress that was a size too small. My expensive satin slippers felt like heavy work boots. I tried to smile, but I was certain everyone could feel what a sham this marriage ceremony was. Rick gave me a polite nod of his head, but I really thought he just looked bored.

Suddenly, standing there at the altar, I couldn't go through with it. When the minister got to the point of asking if I would be faithful and obey this man, I turned, picked up the train of my dress and slung it over an arm, and ran out of the church.

I had taken up jogging just this last summer, finally losing the extra ten pounds I carried for so long. The summer's training got me pretty far down the road on my wedding day, but after about thirty minutes, I finally got winded and stopped, realizing at that moment that it had begun to snow. Though I'd managed to hold the train well enough to take the jog, it was slowing me down. I was grateful I'd chosen long sleeves, but I had no coat, and my feet were killing me. I detached the train and threw it into a bush, along with my veil. Then I slowed to a fast walk. The sun that had shone brightly when I got to the church this morning was now behind a dark cloud that looked like it was holding back a storm. The early snow of the day was replaced by rain, and the cold seeped into my bones and my toes, making me shiver uncontrollably.

After ten minutes more walking, I saw a truck stop and knew I had to stop. My thoughts turned to coffee. Hot, hot coffee. My hand was on the door handle before another thought presented itself: I'm a runaway bride in a dirty wedding gown with no coat, no hat, and, oh yeah, *no money*. People in the coffee shop were likely to think I was a lunatic and call the authorities. I needed warmth, but I couldn't even buy a cup of coffee. I swiveled my head looking at the many semis in the parking lot and decided I just needed shelter and time to think. The first semi was locked up tightly, but the second was open. I climbed up into the cab and flung my body into the front bench. As I hit the leather upholstery, my gaze fell on what was behind the seat: Was that really a mattress and blankets? With some difficulty, I crawled over the front bench, laid my weary bones down and fell asleep.

The phrase, *"What the hell?"* woke me sometime later.

I opened my eyes and my confused brain saw a furry creature bigger than me looming over my resting spot.

"A bear!" I screamed before my brain registered how ridiculous that was.

Instead of being insulted, however, the man laughed.

"A bear am I? What, pray tell are you then…a dirty angel?"

I shook my head to clear it, squinted my eyes and took another look at the guy. He really was a giant of a man with huge shoulders and solid arms, a face covered with black whiskers. His very dark hair was down to his shoulders and completely unruly. In contrast, however, his eyes were a gentle blue that just didn't go along with the rest of the package. "I…I…I was …cold," I stammered, my whole body now shivering. The quaking wasn't from the scare he'd given me—it was from the cold. He reached over the seat and touched my arm and pronounced the obvious: "You're freezing." Then he folded back the front seat, leaned over and scooped me up as if I weighed nothing at all.

"Your dress is wet, your hair is soaked," I heard him grumble as he carried me back towards the diner. Instead of entering it, however, he went past the entrance and walked towards the sign that read: "motel." I knew in that moment I should fight like the dickens, but I just didn't have it in me.

He unlocked the door to a room and put me gently down on one of the beds. I struggled to sit up, but I simply didn't have any energy left. I closed my eyes and tried to think what to do. Then I heard a shower running. He returned to the bed, scooped me up again and deposited me on the closed toilet seat inside the small bathroom, pointing to a pile of towels and saying simply, "Take off your dress. I'll find something for you to wear." Then he turned away and looked like he was about to leave me alone. I stood and my shivering became more violent, now fueled by both cold and fear. "My fingers….I can't….I can't unbutton the pearls."

Suddenly he was back, looming over me and wielding a pocket knife, and I thought, "I'm about to die." Instead, however, he turned me around for access to the back of the dress and with one fluid movement, sliced the fabric, holding it with one hand, then dropping it suddenly as he backed out of the bathroom quickly and shut the door. I knew then I was safe from the giant.

I must have been in that shower for twenty minutes, and it was pure heaven. Slowly, my blood began to warm, my fingers and toes regained feeling, and my mind returned to functioning. I soaped my hair and body, then stood one last time under the spray before turning off the water, grabbing the towel and cracking open the bathroom door—swathed now in a towel gown. He was sitting on the bed, holding a gigantic sweatshirt and a pair of woolen socks. He got up off the bed and handed them over, and I quickly shut the door to dress. The shirt was so long, it fell to my knees, but it was soft and well-worn and smelled smoky like firewood. It must be his natural scent, I thought, and it somehow fits him. I cracked open the bathroom door again.

He was lying on his side facing the wall, and I heard him mutter: "I've driven fifteen hours straight. I have to sleep. Do what you need to do, but you're welcome to stay." Then I heard gentle snores.

I had no idea what to do and stood in that room for about fifteen minutes, yawning and wondering who to call. My eyes kept returning to the other bed in the room and suddenly I made a decision. I crawled under the covers and closed my eyes.

I woke up to the heady aroma of a cup of coffee, and the dawning realization that I was, in fact, a lunatic. I pulled myself up to sit against the head of the bed and look around the room. My gentle giant was nowhere to be seen, but he'd left a Styrofoam cup of coffee and a giant glazed donut sitting on the nightstand. I reached over for both and closed my eyes, savoring the doughy sweetness and hot liquid. How had he managed to guess I liked only milk in my coffee?

Ten minutes later, the motel door opened, and the giant returned. This man had to be almost seven feet tall, I thought, and must weigh 250 pounds—though it appears to be mostly muscle. His hair was combed this morning, but his efforts hadn't done much good—the hair couldn't be tamed. The sleeves of his plaid wool shirt poked out through a downy vest, rolled up on forearms that showed a couple of tattoos. I just couldn't be frightened of someone whose smile was so warm, however. It lit up that hotel room like a lantern.

He handed me a newspaper. "Good morning, Charity Williams," he said, shocking me back to reality.

"How on earth do you know my name?"

"Look at the headlines," he said. His smile dimmed a little.

There was my shameful flight splashed across the front page, but it had a tragic twist: the reporter, who had talked to those in attendance, reported that I must have been kidnapped because I hadn't turned up at my home or anywhere else.

"I don't know what made her run out of that church, but it had to be some kind of threat someone made or a medical condition that rendered her temporarily insane. I know she would not have left me at the altar," Rick told the reporter. "She must have been snatched somewhere outside the church." The story said friends and family at the wedding (which I knew were mostly Rick's) had checked local hospitals and police departments, but no one had seen the bride running in her fancy dress. She'd simply vanished into the afternoon.

I giggled. I just couldn't help it.

"Of course he couldn't fathom I wouldn't go through with it. But *temporary insanity*? I guess, in a way, he was right."

I looked up at my giant. He didn't look angry, but he didn't look particularly happy either.

"Look. My name is Blackjack Murphy, and I'm delighted you chose my truck as a safe haven, but I think maybe you had better call your ex and let him know the truth. I'm not really anxious to be picked up and charged with kidnapping."

He sat down on the opposite bed, and I saw that he held a bag from Wal Mart. He reached inside and withdrew a women's wool shirt, a pair of jeans, a pair of boots and cotton underwear and socks.

"Better put something different on. I didn't know your size, but I tried. That sweatshirt of mine is cute on you, but hardly appropriate for the outside."

The clothes looked like they might fit, which astounded me. I returned to the bathroom and wiggled into the jeans, surprised that they were a size smaller than I usually wore. They fit. Guess the lost ten pounds had caught up to me, and I hadn't even realized it because I seldom wore something as tight as jeans. I returned to sit on the bed opposite where he sat. He looked like he wanted to talk, and I thought uh oh. He's finally realized he has a nut in his care.

But all he said was: "You have a decision you need to make."

I crossed my arms and sat back, sighing heavily. I didn't really want to think about the botched wedding.

"What decision must I make?" I asked.

"What are you going to do now?" he said.

I hung my head, trying to think, then lifted it to gaze into the gentleness of his eyes.

"Where are you headed next?" I asked.

He lifted his eyebrows but didn't ask why I was inquiring. Since I didn't know why I *had* asked, I was relieved.

"Atlanta, Georgia to deliver my cargo," he said.

"And is there a wife waiting for you at the end of the road?" Now, why had I asked *that* question?

He laughed. "Not anymore. My wife couldn't take my size, my occupation or my charming beard. The only woman waiting for me is my eight-year-old daughter, who doesn't get to see me very often. This is my weekend with her, and I'm picking her up for ice cream as soon as I drop off my load."

I squirmed, and I thought, and I scratched my chin while the gentle giant and his lovely blue eyes just kept staring at me. Suddenly, I was sick of being Charity Williams, poor little rich girl with the tree trunk body. I was also sick of always doing the proper thing; acting the way people expected; taking the easy road until someone like Rick came along to shake it all up.

"Mind if I tag along for the ride?" The words came out easily enough, but I saw the look on Blackjack Murphy's face. It wasn't shock, but it wasn't acceptance. He was weighing if indeed, I was crazy.

"I've never been to Atlanta," I continued. "I've never ridden in a semi. I don't know many eight-year-old bear cubs. And I really like ice cream."

Blackjack's laughter seemed to break the spell of heaviness. It was deep and resonating, like the bass violin underlying a good string ensemble. When it finally died down, the room was suddenly filled with an echoing silence. He drew his phone out of a breast pocket and I thought: is he thinking now about whether to call the authorities?

He handed it to me instead.

"Okay, little one," he said. "It's on to Atlanta for us both. But you need to make a few calls before we hit the road. I don't want any state troopers spotting my 'hostage.'"

And that's the end of this chapter of my story—but also the beginning of the rest of it. That was the very moment I fell in love. I became hooked on this man, and it's a feeling that has stayed with me for thirty-five years. All I ever have to do is think back on the time he called me "little one" and handed me his phone, and I get the same warm feeling I did then; the same moment of clarity. I knew, without a doubt, that this was the man I was going to marry. It took a while for it to happen, but I was right. The gentle bear had rescued this little one from herself.

Twinkles from Heaven

by Allyn M. Stotz

(For DeAnn)

I looked to the stars for answers, but all I got were more questions.

Why are you so beautiful and yet you seem to have no purpose? All you do is twinkle. You can't talk, you can't give me a hug, you can't solve problems. Why are you even up there?

I knew I was being ridiculous, but I was in a bad mood. I was taking my frustrations out on something that couldn't fight back. If I complained to my dog instead, she'd tilt her head like usual, an expression that said, "Look, Mom, are you losing your mind again? You know I can't answer back!"

If my husband was home, he'd be my target, even though his response was usually to roll over on the couch and go back to sleep.

So instead of taking it out on either of the other living souls in my home, I'd chosen the sky. I walked inside, refilled my glass of wine and was returning to talk to the glittering stars when the ring of my cell phone stopped me.

"Hello," I answered.

"Charlene, It's Mike Tilly. Megan's son."

"Oh hi, Michael. This is an unexpected surprise. How's your family? How's your mom?"

Mike said nothing for a moment then cleared his throat. "I'm afraid I have some very bad news."

I switched my cell phone to the other ear and sat down. "What? Is it your ma? Is she all right?"

"No, she's not. There was a horrible accident on Route 6 this morning. Mom was killed."

I couldn't speak. I couldn't move. Megan had been my best friend since high school. She and I chatted yesterday about how lucky we were to finally have grandchildren in our lives. *I didn't hear him right, that's all.*

"I'm sorry, Michael, did you say your mom was in an accident? Please tell me I heard you wrong."

Michael's tone was steady, but I could hear the strain to keep it that way. "You heard right, Miss Charlene. Mom was killed instantly"

"Oh, Mike. I'm so sorry."

My words must have broken the last of his resolve. I heard him gasp, and his voice became shaky. "I don't know what we're going to do. I haven't been able to tell the kids yet. They'll be devastated. They loved Granny Meg so much."

I felt the pull to join Mike in his grief. I wanted to scream. I needed to pound something. But letting go wouldn't help my godson. I rubbed a hand across my forehead, trying to steady myself.

"Michael, you and Mona are raising those kids to be strong. They'll make it through this, and I'll help. Daniel and I will be there as soon as we can get a flight out."

We talked for a few more horrible minutes, both of us trying desperately to get control of our emotions. Both failing at times. The only good thing that came from our words back and forth was that I learned Megan probably hadn't known what happened. The crash was extensive but occurred quickly. Megan never saw it coming.

As soon as I pushed "end," I crumbled to the floor.

"No! Megan can't be gone!" I finally yelled. "She's a good person; she doesn't deserve this!"

I'm not sure how long I crouched on the cold tile floor, my head in my lap. I was only aware of pain. In my knees, in my head, in my stomach and most of all, deep in my heart. I felt my body trembling and began gasping for air. I thought I'd just die right there, but that wouldn't be so bad. Then I wouldn't have to deal with the days ahead of me.

The feel of a wet, clammy tongue on my face brought me back to the present.

"My sweet darling Beemer. I'm the luckiest mom to have you for my dog. You always know when I need you, don't you Baby?"

Beemer licked my face and darted to the back door to ring the bell. That was my cue she needed to go outside. I pushed myself into a standing position and cursed.

"Of all nights for Daniel to be out of town, I need him here right now, helping me with this pain. At least he could've let the dog out for me." I knew how petty that sounded. I didn't care. I opened the door for Beemer, then stepped out after him.

I looked toward the stars and shook my fist. *"Good for nothing sparkles. Just go away!"*

The weeks passed in a haze of grief and activity. Daniel and I flew back to Ohio for Megan's funeral, but I couldn't come to grips with the reality. I walked around like a zombie, helping with funeral arrangements, watching Michael and Mona's kids, cleaning and cooking for the family, visiting with old friends, talking endlessly about what happened but never quite believing it. How could my best friend be gone? Every single morning, I thought about calling her. But there would be no more phone calls and no more late-night conversations trying to solve the world's problems. I hadn't a clue how I would make it through the rest of my life without her.

I was there in Ohio for several weeks. Being back in my hometown area made me feel closer to her, but it also made me question why I now lived in Florida. I always hated the hot weather. I didn't particularly care for the terrain. We'd just ended up there.

Daniel and I had moved to Florida when we were a young couple and the kids were very small. We'd been seeking a new adventure—the beaches and sun—but we'd also believed it would be a great place to raise our kids, and we'd been right. Our kids had been happy down South.

However, as often happens in life, circumstances drew us apart and neither kid ended up there. Our son Chad met and married a wonderful girl but moved to Tennessee to be near her family. We visited him often on our way to or from Ohio, back in the days when both sets of grandparents were still alive. During one of those frequent trips, Michelle met her husband-to-be. It was hard for us when she married Tim and moved back to Ohio, but her family seemed to love it.

While it had been great having Michelle and her family so close to my hometown and my best friend, it was always painful and sad to say goodbye.

Being back this time for the funeral made me wonder why Daniel and I couldn't come back this way for good. Daniel was a writer by trade. There was no reason why we couldn't just pick up now and move wherever we wanted.

When we finally made it back to Florida after Megan's funeral, I paced the floors of the house I'd lived in for thirty-six years and thought of the arguments I'd use to convince Daniel to go back permanently. We didn't need to stay for my job; I had retired from a long human resources career. Why shouldn't we be close to our daughter, our grandchildren and our old friends?

Ringing in my ears, though, were what I imagined Daniel's concerns would be. He loved living in Florida. He hated cold weather. He wouldn't want to leave the writing group he belonged to and dearly loved. And what about poker nights with his buddies? Could he find those things back in our small town?

I grabbed my cell phone and hit the speed dial. Then I dropped it to the ground and raised my palm to stare at my hand, as though the phone had been boiling hot. Collapsing into the nearest chair, I covered my face with both hands. Megan was no longer there to talk me through these things. I had to figure this out all on my own now.

That evening after dinner, I looked over at Daniel, who was engrossed in a TV documentary I'd found particularly boring, and decided it was time to broach the subject.

My hands were sweating, my voice shaky, but I managed to mutter "Can we move back to Ohio?"

Daniel gazed at me wide-eyed, his mind probably still on *The Planes that Helped Us Win World War II*. "Did you say something?"

You can do this, my internal cheerleader said.

"I've been thinking we should move back to Ohio," I said, my voice now calm. "I miss our daughter and grandkids. Wouldn't it be great to see them grow up and attend their school events? You could start a new poker group with some of your old buddies, and I'm sure there's a writer's group in the area. If only…"

Daniel stood up and came to me. He grabbed both my hands and pulled me up from my chair.

"We've been married way too long. You're reading my mind again. I want to move back home, too. I've already researched the writing opportunities nearby, and it looks promising. Let's go for it! There's nothing holding us here."

I hugged this man I loved deeply. "I knew I married you for a reason."

Then I let him go, grabbed Beemer and snuggled her as well. "Beemer, we're going on a new adventure!"

For the next few years, we doubled our trips back to Ohio so we could house hunt. Michelle hooked us up with Harley, a talented realtor she knew. However, the market wasn't great right then for small towns so finding a house for sale, much less one that satisfied our tastes and desires, wasn't easy. We were used to living in the big city where tons of homes were available that were modern and spacious. In my small town, everything seemed old and in need of repair or not big enough. We were definitely spoiled.

We even thought about giving up. The extra trips back and forth were getting to be too much on us physically as well as hard on our pocketbook. Michelle suggested we move in with her for a few months so we could really sink our teeth into looking without worrying about expenses so much, but we just couldn't do it.

Finally, though, after many conversations with our realtor, she found us a house on the outskirts of town that sounded perfect. A visit home confirmed it. The house had been recently renovated. The kitchen was huge and would be great for family get-togethers. The upstairs had a loft that was perfect for Daniel's writing hours. But one of the things I loved most about the house was the backyard. It had a swing on the back porch just like I always dreamed of having. I knew if we bought this property, I would spend many hours there.

After days of playing the bidding war, the sellers accepted our offer. Feeling overjoyed and completely confident of what we were doing, we quickly sold our home in Florida and within a few months, moved to Ohio.

Even though the house was newly updated, we still needed to do some painting to satisfy our tastes. I was jamming out to music, on my knees painting trim inside one of the closets when I noticed something. Sticking out from under the edge of the carpet we'd just pulled up to paint the trim was a piece of paper. I had to work it out of the carpet carefully not to tear it to shreds. The note had definitely been lodged there beneath the rug for a while. I smoothed out the wrinkles and read:

"Granny, I miss you so much. Why did you go? I look at the sky every night wishing I could see you. Last night I saw the biggest star in the sky twinkling right at me so bright. I know it was you telling me hello and that you're safe in heaven. Thank you, Granny. Love, Meggie."

I pulled the earphones out of my ears and read the note again. Something about the childish scrawl pulled at my heartstrings. I gave up my painting task and went to sit on the bed, then read the note again. By the time Daniel walked in, I was in tears, but didn't really understand why. "What's wrong, hon? What are you reading?"

I showed him what I'd found. He thought it was sweet but didn't understand why I was crying. I really didn't either.

The next morning, I asked Harley to stop by the house, saying I had something I thought the previous owners might like back.

She read it slowly, nodding her head. "That is so thoughtful of you, Charlene. But I believe the previous owners didn't have any children. I imagine this note was from the owners before that. I think they were the Tillys, who moved out of town to the new development on Route 6. You know: the ones who lost their daughter Megan a couple years ago in a horrific car accident. Meggie might be Megan when she was little."

I gasped and felt my eyes bulge.

"Are you all right, Charlene? *Charlene*!"

"What did you just say—about the Tillys. You said the Tillys lived here?"

"Yes. It was a long time ago, I know. They lived here when Megan was in elementary school before the family moved out to Route 6."

I folded up the note and put it in a pocket. "Do you think it would be okay if I keep this note then? I knew Megan Tilly very well."

"I'm sure its fine, Charlene."

After she left, I sat down at my kitchen table stunned and slightly numb. I had no clue where Megan lived before I met her in high school. I knew her as one of the kids who arrived by bus. My family was townies, but hers must have been when she was little. How could it have happened that

I ended up in the house where she lived as a child?

I took out the note, smoothed it out again and read the words several times before holding the paper close to my heart. Suddenly, I knew what to do.

The cemetery in town was filled with names I recognized from my days in the area. I found Megan's grave and sat close to it, talking to her at length. I told her about finding the note. About how much I missed her. I reminisced about our days in high school, the many late night talks we'd had over the years. Then I buried the note in front of her stone.

I felt a sense of peace I hadn't felt since the night my best friend died—the night I'd stop gazing at the stars wondering how they could twinkle when life was so hard. Megan had given me the answer.

That weekend, my grandchild Becky spent the night with us. We sat on the back porch swinging together.

"Look, Grandma, there are so many stars out tonight!" She pointed skyward. "That big sparkly one is blinking off and on like it wants to come out of the sky and visit us. You think it does? It's so pretty. I love stars."

My throat was tight, but I got the words out. "I do too, honey… I do too."

One in the Bush

Genilee Swope Parente

A movement in the nearby bushes caught Paul's eye, and he realized he'd been so absorbed in his dark thoughts, his brain hadn't registered a whimpering sound coming from that area.

He'd been too wrapped up in his own anger to pay attention. Paul had just learned he was unemployed: He'd lost the position he'd fought so hard to get. "Downsizing." "Online migration." "Budget cuts." What did it matter? It all meant the dream job was gone, a job he'd gotten after practically stalking the magazine's executive editor, finally connecting with her at a coffee shop and convincing her he was the right guy for the position.

The whimpers from the bush grew louder, and Paul finally got up from the park bench as much out of irritation as concern. He parted the branches and discovered a shivering mutt that shrank further into the bush when its frightened eyes connected with Paul's angry ones.

"I don't know what your problem is, but I can't help you if you're too chicken to come out," Paul said.

The dog didn't move so Paul shrugged his shoulders and returned to the bench.

He had to figure out what to do about the job situation. Jalissa was already upset with him for accepting the position in the first place.

"You have an advanced accounting degree, for God's sake. A job with the best firm in town. Why in the world would you exchange it for long hours and lousy pay at some business magazine no one's ever heard of?"

Because at 33, I'm turning to dust! He'd wanted to scream at her. But screaming was more her style than his. He'd kept quiet knowing she'd never understand how much he wanted to write; how much he *needed* to write. At the same time, he also knew she'd eventually accept the reality of the new job, despite lower pay and more hours. A career switch wouldn't be a deal-breaker in their relationship. She was too settled into his apartment and his life to walk out the door because of a pay cut.

How will she react to this latest development though? No job at all. Paul rubbed his face with both hands then dropped them to his side, almost knocking the food bag off the bench. He'd stormed out of the office after getting the bad news, not knowing exactly where he was going. Out of habit and the fact it was lunchtime, he'd stopped for a sub, but he wasn't in the least bit hungry. Paul gazed at the bush. Maybe the mutt was whining because it had smelled the food.

Paul opened the bag and tore off a piece of salami, then approached the bush again. Instead of parting the leaves, he simply stuck his hand into the bush not even caring about a possible dog bite. What the hell; he had insurance for another month—he could afford to get rabies. But instead of a chomp, he felt a gentle tug. The dog was taking the salami.

Paul went back to the bench, got the food bag and tore off more meat. He laid the pieces just outside the bush and trailed them back toward the bench. His action was more an experiment than an act of kindness. He needed a distraction.

It took about five minutes, but eventually, a small pink nose appeared out of the greenness. It twitched a bit as the scent caught hold, and eventually, an entire muzzle and head appeared out of the leaves.

God what an ugly mutt, Paul thought. He sat back down on the bench to watch as more of the dog emerged. The fur looked like steel wool—wiry and not quite curly—almost the same grey color as scouring pads before Jalissa put them to work and turned them soapy blue.

As the dog got closer, picking up each piece carefully and chewing slowly, never tearing its caramel-colored gaze away from Paul's face, he realized the grey came from a layer of dirt that covered her sparse coat—and that the filth didn't hide the scrawny outline of the dog's frame. *This animal has obviously been lost awhile*, Paul thought.

Half an hour later, Paul regretted sharing his sandwich with the dog. The mutt had never quite made it to the bench and returned to the bush after the food was gone. Paul headed for home knowing his boss would understand he needed time to clear his head. He wasn't aware the animal was behind him until he was close to his own doorway and heard a sharp yap. The sound made him turn backward where he saw the little grey dog sitting on her haunches a few yards behind him.

"What the …? Where did you come from?" Paul asked.

The mutt tilted her head.

"Look, fluffy or doodles or whatever the heck your name is … you can't live with me. Jalissa is allergic to pet hair and neither of us needs to be walking a dog every day or cleaning up dog doodoo. Besides, she has enough motive to murder me without me bringing home a dirty mongrel." Paul wondered why he felt the need to explain to an animal what his situation was. He turned back around and got out his key.

"Yip yip. *Yip.*"

It isn't even a real bark, Paul thought. He inserted the key and turned it, then cracked the door, prepared to dash in and close it quickly before the dog could dart inside with him.

"Arf. *Arf.*"

Paul grinned and turned back around.

"Okay, so you can bow wow properly. I'm not that impressed though. And I really do *not* want a dog."

He made little shooing gestures and stamped his foot, but the dog did not move. She tilted her head the other way and this time, when Paul turned to his door, her barking became frantic. Did the little thing have it in her to attack?

Paul ignored her and opened the door wider, but saw almost immediately that something was amiss. A lamp lay broken on its side and the mail that was usually just inside his door was opened and scattered about. He heard a crash and knew that someone that didn't belong inside his house was making that sound. Had the pup been trying to warn him? He stepped back outside and called the police.

"You did the right thing, calling us and leaving," Officer David Williams said between scratches on his pad. "These guys have hit a half dozen houses in the area and there's no telling how they would have reacted to someone coming in on them in the middle of their mischief."

It was a lot more than mischief, Paul thought as he looked around the apartment.

The 55-inch television was gone; several glass vases were broken and scattered on the floor, drawers had been emptied. The thieves were obviously not quiet cat burglars. They were there to grab and go. Paul's gaze fell on the dog. She had stayed close to his side as he made the call, then waited at his neighbor's stoop for the cruisers to arrive and trotted in as if she lived with Paul when he was allowed back into his home. The thieves had escaped out the back, taking Jalissa's few precious pieces of jewelry, the cash he kept stashed for poker games, his iPad and whatever else they could get. They'd left the television outside the back door, too awkward a treasure to carry once their departure became hasty. The cracked screen mocked Paul, who been meaning to put in an alarm system for months now.

I guess the dog was my own personal alarm, he thought. He was grateful he hadn't walked into the house, and he figured he owed the dog at least a meal and maybe a bath for warning him. After that, he'd call some kind of rescue place. This dog deserved a home.

He should have realized Jalissa wouldn't feel the same—wouldn't think he owed an animal anything, even if it had prevented him from harm. She arrived home three hours after Paul, prepared by a phone call for the aftereffects of the theft. For some reason, however, his call to her hadn't included an explanation about the dog or his lost job. He thought he'd ease her into those additional negative developments.

She stood now at the bathroom mirror, mascara wand waving in one hand as she aired her displeasure.

"You cannot use my good towels on a flea-infested mongrel," she said as he prepared to take the little dog out of the tub.

"I'll use the rags from the washroom," I said.

Jalissa sneezed and laid down the mascara on the sink then turned to stomp out of the bathroom. Paul was glad it was book club night, and that she'd probably be gone longer than normal. The burglary and the dog would provide much fodder for the wine-sipping members of her club. He needed some extra time to think about how he would break the news about his job.

Paul picked up one of the good towels from the dirty clothes bin and began rubbing the dog. Jalissa would never know he'd used it if he threw in a load of wash tonight.

Paul got up from his knees, stretched and took a step back to study the mutt. "Well, now, you're not so ugly when you remove the grey, little one," he murmured to the dog. He wondered if she was some kind of mix of poodle and maybe a rat terrier. She was all bones when wetted down, but the fur was surprisingly white and soft with a few spots of brown that matched the pretty brown of her expressive eyes. Though shivering from the trauma of a bath, the dog had been complacent while he washed her, which made Paul wonder if she'd had an owner who regularly bathed her. What had happened to that person? Maybe he would put up a few fliers and try to find the dog's true home.

Paul knew finding the owner might require some time, and Jalissa would not be happy caring for a dog, even if it was a temporary situation. He sighed and lifted the dog out of the bath to the floor where she proceeded to shake violently, emitting a stream of water that hit him in the face and shoulders but made him laugh.

As he walked down the hall to the kitchen, the dog followed behind, toenails clicking on the tiled floor. When Paul got to the kitchen, he stood at the open refrigerator wondering what a dog could eat besides sandwich meat. He took out a hunk of cheese, grabbed some crackers for himself from atop the frig and extracted a knife from the kitchen block, then sat down at the table. The dog followed him back and forth between frig and table, and Paul wondered why she hadn't yet wandered away to explore the rest of the house. *Must be a hungry pup.* She also didn't try to jump onto a chair or yap to be fed as Paul cut some of the cheese off. Instead of popping it into his mouth, he held it out to his new friend. A delicate pink tongue came out to lick the food and finally, take the offering. The tongue came back out to lick the hand that had fed her.

Paul laughed again.

"I'll get you some more, little one, so don't eat my hand!"

Paul decided he'd called her Kelly Girl because of her status as a temporary guest. He knew Jalissa was too young to get the reference to post-World War II temporary employees, and she was not a lover of either history or trivia. He doubted the term had ever crept up on "The Real Housewives of Atlanta."

Later that night, as Paul made up a makeshift bed from an old blanket, he tried to tune out the barrage of Jalissa's objections. Her pretty pout, which often got her what she wanted, just couldn't counteract her cross words at finding the dog still there when she got home.

"Geesus, Paul. How could you let that thing stay here? It probably has fleas or mange. They have people that will take strays you know. Why didn't you just call the pound?"

"It's not an 'it.' It's a girl. I did call the pound and sent them a picture to post on their site. But they said I was more likely to find the owners if I posted notices around the neighborhood where I found her. And they're not a no-kill facility. I put my cell number on the flier, and I'm sure someone will call."

Paul wondered why he was bothering to explain. Jalissa was madder about the dog than she'd been when he finally told her he'd lost his job. Or maybe it was just the straw on the camel's back. As he lay on his side, staring at the wall opposite him, her harsh words scratched at his usually calm surface.

"It was tough enough having your income cut nearly in half when you took that dang writers job, and now we have to squeak by just on my paycheck," she said as she climbed into bed, pulled the covers towards her and lay down facing away from him. "I don't see why I have to give up everything because you can't keep a decent job …," she grumbled.

The next few days were much the same: Jalissa was like the leaky faucet that just wouldn't shut up. But Paul knew her. He clammed up, knowing the sounds would eventually fade. He didn't feel the need to point out *again* that he owned the house they were living in outright—an inheritance from his grandmother. He didn't feel the need to explain *again* that he had savings or that he wasn't unemployable. The magazine had given him two week's notice—he could do a lot of job hunting in that amount of time—and two more weeks of severance pay.

Paul knew Jalissa's tirades would eventually run out of steam so he stuck to a daily routine to get through his days, rising before work to send out resumes, coming home to continue the job search and then taking an hour or two before bed to enjoy his temporary canine companion.

He didn't see much of his girlfriend, who spent most nights going out with friends—punishing him for his sins. Even when he banned Kelly Girl to the hallway at night, Jalissa pushed Paul away and continued to grumble. He was becoming accustomed to the sound of her rants mixed with the sound of Kelly Girl whining softly outside the bedroom door. He couldn't blame either gal: Jalissa really didn't want a dog around; Kelly Girl had finally found a friend, but the friend locked her out at night.

"It's just plain creepy if you ask me," Jalissa muttered. "It's like that dog is in love with you."

But Paul wasn't afraid she'd ever present an ultimatum: the dog or me. She didn't have the guts for that.

Three weeks went by, no one answered the posted fliers, no one called from the pound and Paul was at home during the day for the first time in years. He guessed he should have been depressed, but Kelly Girl became his daytime cheerleader, and Jalissa's nighttime complaining had dwindled to almost nothing. The gloom he could have felt by being without a job was counterbalanced by long walks during the day with his new friend. The weather had softened with the coming Spring, and Paul felt his mind and his muscles relax as if he'd been wound too tightly before all this happened, and he was just being let free of his cage. He guessed he didn't realize that, despite the fact he loved working for a magazine, the job had been stressful. He'd loved every minute of the writing—profiles of people that fascinated him, topics that absorbed his mind, long afternoons and nights of stringing together words and then polishing them. But the constant pressure to meet deadlines, the toughness of his boss were always there in the background.

The walks with Kelly Girl cleared away the dark clouds and allowed his dreams to break through. The two of them—canine and canine protector—often returned to the bench where they'd met to "discuss" the status of Paul's life.

"What about trying to use both my backgrounds and maybe writing for an accounting publication?" he asked his new pal.

Kelly Girl gave a low-throated growl and laid her head on her paws.

Paul laughed.

"Okay. Maybe that was a really stupid idea. But I don't want to give up writing just to make the money I need."

Kelly Girl's head raised from her paws and her beautiful brown eyes looked straight into his soul.

"You think I need to make writing the priority and money the second?" he asked. She gave a bark of approval.

Paul fell back against the bench, intertwined his fingers and put his hands behind his head. He felt the sun beating on his forehead and raised his face to take in the warmth. The beginning of an idea was forming.

Paul spent the rest of that afternoon cooking. It had been too long since he'd shared an actual meal with Jalissa at home.

When she wasn't out with friends, she'd been putting in extra hours to try to bring in some cushion money, and he was truly grateful for the effort. He'd managed to save enough in his years in accounting not to be really worried they'd run out of money, but he knew she felt better with padding. He also knew he was better at managing other people's bottom line than his own. He'd never be a millionaire.

Jalissa deserved to be thanked for her efforts, and he'd splurged for a good bottle of red to go along with the flank steak he was preparing. He hoped the wine would relax her a bit; open her up so they could talk. He wanted to share with her his decision to become a freelance writer while writing a book. It wouldn't pay well, but it was a definite step in the right direction: toward a future doing what he needed to do.

In his short time with the magazine, he knew his byline had already been noticed around town, and he'd established quite a few contacts with places he knew used freelancers. Meanwhile, he would sit down every day for at least an hour to work on his book.

The aroma of the meat was so enticing, Kelly Girl had plopped down under a kitchen chair and not moved while he prepped the potatoes and cut the salad. Paul heard the front door open.

"I'm in the kitchen, Jal Gal. A special treat is in store …"

He turned from the counter to see her standing at the kitchen door, a bedraggled figure beaten down by the rain as well as a long day. She looked from him to the dog and finally settled her gaze on the oven.

"I made your favorite. Flank steak and baby rosemary potatoes …"

His words didn't seem to penetrate. She turned and walked down the hall towards their bedroom, throwing her wet raincoat onto the coat rack in the process.

Paul sought out the caramel gaze of his canine friend under the chair.

"Well, that bodes poorly," he said.

Kelly Girl just yawned.

Paul turned off the oven, took the dish towel off his shoulder and put it on the counter. He made his way down the hallway to find Jalissa packing her bags.

"Going somewhere?"

"… leaving you. Met someone else. Staying with Jane for a while. The dog wins. We have no future."

Paul only heard bits and pieces. He wasn't really surprised by anything she said, and he knew she was right about it all. He'd been so absorbed in his thoughts about what to do with his life, he hadn't really given their relationship full consideration lately. While he'd told himself the dinner was a step towards renewal, he knew it had also been about missing having someone besides a dog to share those thoughts.

Paul sat down on the bed and watched her grab drawers full of clothes and stuff them into a suitcase. She obviously hadn't thought the actual move through—she'd just reached some kind of limit. In fact, he was proud of her for acting on impulse for once. He supposed he'd wake up tomorrow with some regrets, but for the moment he just felt relief.

Paul made no comment, no appeals and no excuses as Jalissa continued to mumble and pack. When she was done, he helped her lug her suitcases to the front room and then outside the door. *Someone must be picking her up,* he thought, because she kept glancing at her fit bit for the time.

When the last of the cases was outside and Jalissa had shrugged into her discarded coat and thrown the keys at Paul, he went into the kitchen and opened the wine. He turned the oven back on and sat. As he heard the front door slam a final time, Paul leaned down to pet Kelly Girl's head.

"Looks like its just you and me now, Kid. I think I can live with that."

Dream Date

Christina Parente

(For Robert Bausch, an extraordinary teacher and storyteller)

I stare out the window at the beautiful autumn day. Beyond the train tracks across from our office is a meadow. The sun shines down on the fallen leaves, stirring up images of my puppy Laney, who loves to run on the crunchy "carpet." I see her in pursuit of rabbits, her beagle ears flopping, her tongue hanging out of her mouth. If she were there now outside my window, she'd be crouched down, rooting through the leaves with her nose, following the scent of something exciting. In my vision, she is just about to catch one when…

"Ana… Anaaaaa! Hellooooo??" a masculine voice bellows.

"Oh, Alec! Didn't see you there! What's up?" I say to the cute guy standing by my desk.

"Glad you could join us, Mizz Space Cadet. Ed wants you to process this paperwork right away. The base is asking for it. Apparently, the customer is some top-ranked officer and he's throwing a fit."

Alec's pretty blue eyes roll heavenward.

"Don't they all?" I say.

"Yep," he agrees, with his brilliantly white smile. "Hey! You look nice today by the way. Are you going to happy hour with everyone after work?"

"Oh gee, yeah, probably. I don't have anything better to do."

I can feel the blood rushing to my cheeks. *A compliment from Alec? He wants to know if I'm going to happy hour? Guess this morning's extra ten minutes at the mirror was worth it.*

"Cool! See you there!" Alec walks away, and all I can think is… *damn. He's hot!*

I'm walking to my car after work, thinking of the possibilities of that happy hour. I've had a crush on Alec since the first day we met—he gave me a fist bump and made me laugh in the first fifteen seconds of knowing me, and I've been smitten ever since. But we haven't spent much time together and never away from the office.

Maybe, with a little liquid courage, I'll be able to ask him to hang out. I've been meaning to for a while now, but every time I'm about there, I choke up. *Just form the sentence in your head and don't get tongue tied,* I say to myself whenever I'm close to his desk. However, I get nauseous and my vision blurs, and I find myself using the excuse that we're at work where nosy people are always lingering, hoping for a chance to get into everyone else's business. That excuse has kept me from opening my mouth. It hasn't kept me from praying he'd walk by my desk just so I can talk to him though.

"Hey, Ana! Wait up!" the very guy I'm thinking about shouts. I turn around to find Alec sprinting across the parking lot.

"What's up, dude?" *Dude…?? Why the heck did I call him dude? What is wrong with me?*

"I was just wondering… Would you maybe want to ride with me to the bar? It'd be nice to have company, and you're always saying you want a ride in my truck. I figured this would be the perfect opportunity."

"Yeah, of course!" I say, trying hard not to sound excited. "Let me just grab a few things from my car, and I'll be right over." Despite my resolve to remain calm, I practically run to that car, then give up all pretense of cool and calm as I hurry back. I can't get in his truck fast enough; I can't believe he offered a ride.

I jump up into the cab and roll down my window.

"I hope you don't mind; it's just so nice outside. I'd hate to miss it," I say.

"A girl after my own heart," Alec says. His mouth slants in that crooked smile I've come to adore.

We drive down Route One, laughing and tossing out stories about our job and our coworkers. Elton John's "Bennie and the Jets" comes on the radio, and we look at each other, then burst into song simultaneously. I'm impressed that he knows it word for word, just like me. I silently thank my dad for introducing me to this type of music.

We arrive at the bar and jump out of the truck. As we walk toward the door, Alec grasps my wrist to stop me.

"Wait… before we go in there…" He turns me around, and I can see anticipation in his eyes as well as a tinge of something that looks almost like trepidation. *What could he possibly have to be afraid of or nervous about?*

"I've been meaning to ask you for a while…Would you want to go see a movie sometime?"

"Alec Stevens… are you asking me on a date?" I tease, trying to put him at ease.

He just stares at me. Waiting for an answer?

"I don't know man… I have a pretty busy schedule, and I just don't think I can fit you in anywhere," I say.

"Oh, I see, well…" Alec turns away, and I can't believe I saw disappointment on his face.

"I'm just kidding! I've been wanting to ask you the same thing! I would love to!" I say. I throw my arms around him for a quick, reassuring hug. As I'm pulling away, I look into his face ... so close to me. I feel his finger lift my chin, and he slowly brings his lips toward me. Just before he brings the kiss home, I turn and walk away, looking over a shoulder with what I hope is a playful look. "You're gonna have to put some work in before you get one of those!"

He gets the joke, smiles at me and chases me inside.

We spot friends in the corner of the bar by the dart boards. I walk over to one of my favorite coworkers Candice, who is smiling broadly.

"You little rascal you!" she whispers. "How'd you con your way into a ride with Mr. Alec over there?"

"Candice, I didn't con him! He offered. Being the polite lady I am, I wasn't going to say 'no.' That's just rude! My parents raised me better than that."

Candice laughs and picks up some darts, handing me the red set.

As the night wears on, Alec and I find many reasons to stand close together. We play a round of darts, have a few drinks, talk about our lives. But we also mingle with our friends, knowing now that we'll have time together later. At some point, we are at different ends of the bar, and I catch him staring at me. He quickly looks away, but I see his embarrassment at being caught. It gives me a warm and wonderful feeling.

"You know I've never seen him act this way." I jump at Candice's voice. I didn't know she was standing behind me.

"Candice, geesus! Let a girl know you're walking up behind her. What are you talking about anyway?" I say.

"I've worked with Alec for years. We've gone to happy hour at least once a week. I've never seen him be so… attentive, yet relaxed."

"What do you mean, Candice? I'm sure he always has girls hanging on him."

"Oh, sure. I mean look at him!" she says, pointing her glass towards the other end of the bar. "If I wasn't married to my wife, I'd totally go for him!" She winks. "You're a lucky girl Ana."

"I am," I say, turning back to study Alec again.

Later, he asks me to dance, and surprisingly, I say 'yes.' I've never been confident on the dance floor; I'm what you would call a seat dancer. However, Alec makes me feel comfortable, beautiful, confident all at once. The song "Stairway to Heaven" comes on, a song that reminds me of my parents—it's the tune playing the night they met, and later the song they had their first dance to as a married couple. I look up at Alec and stare into his eyes, deciding the blue goes beyond the standard ocean grey/blue to mimic the blue/green of a sea. *I can't believe this is really happening to me.*

The lights in the bar begin to flicker.

"*Last call!*" the bartender shouts.

Alec and I break away from each other to say our goodbyes to our coworkers.

We walk to his truck, and he opens the door. I do a theater curtsy and giggle. He shakes his head and laughs.

As we are driving back to the office and my car, he reaches across my lap and grabs my hand. I look at him and just smile, knowing he doesn't need to see that smile. He'll feel it. He keeps his eyes on the road like a good driver.

It gives me a moment to study his features, trying to imprint the image on my mind. His short autumn brown hair is just a bit curly; his somewhat pointy ears connect to a chiseled jaw in elf-like fashion. His eyebrows furrow just a little bit as he concentrates on the road. His small, plump lips are pursed. I turn my eyes away to look out at the road, needing a moment to let my thoughts settle. This really has been the night of my dreams.

We get to the parking lot, and Alec jumps out of the car to come around and open my door in an old-fashioned charming gesture. He gives me a hand to help me out of the car. He squeezes that hand and pulls me in for a hug. We pull away slowly and I can feel, finally, that he is about to kiss me. He leans close, I crave those enticing lips and lose myself in those twinkling eyes. I close my eyes, ready to feel his mouth against mine and I hear: "Ana… Anaaaaa! Hellooooo?"

What the heck? My eyes fly open.

"Ana, are you daydreaming again?" Alec asks.

I shake my head and look around me, confused for a moment, until I realize: I've done it again… I've been staring out my office window, lost in my fantasies. I'm sitting here at my desk.

I can't believe it.

My dream date was just that… a really good daydream.

A Friend Comes Home

Mark Swope

*I*t's really happening. *After all this time, I can finally see him again and start to give back.*

I shift my weight off my prosthetic leg, trying to get comfortable. I still have trouble standing for long periods of time, even after months and months of recovery. I do my stretches and think about sitting, but I'm just too restless and anxious for the plane to arrive.

He saved me in so many ways. I'll never be able to repay the debt I owe, but at least now I can try.

I rub my eyes. My excitement kept me from sleeping last night and adrenaline drove me out of bed well before the alarm went off. I distracted myself this morning every way I could think of, but arrived forty-five minutes ahead of the flight anyway. I stand now outside of airport security waiting for the friend I haven't seen in nearly two years.

Will he still feel the same way about me? Will he even remember me?

I need to calm down, so I find a bench and sit. There is still at least twenty minutes before the plane is scheduled to touch down. The wait gives me time to think, something I've had way too much of in the last year. But instead of focusing on the fact it has been the toughest year of my life, a time spent fighting depression and battle fatigue, then learning to walk on a stump and fake leg, my thoughts travel to the past.

I grew up an Army brat, moving every few years from town to town as Dad's job required. Those moves were a frequent subject during this last year's therapy sessions. My doctor was trying to help me figure out why I found it so difficult to make friends.

Why make friends when you won't be around long? This had been the thinking he'd helped me pinpoint.

I talked a lot with the doctor about my first real friendship: Rick, who I met during my freshman year of high school. I guess you could say our mutual love of animals threw us together and enabled us to bond during the few years my family spent in Hampton, Virginia. It was one of only a handful of places where my parents bought a house. Because we had the house, they decided to get me a dog, which I named Apollo.

I took my furry friend to the dog park near our new house frequently to toss a ball. On one of those trips, a Collie came bounding over to greet us, his tongue hanging loose, his ears flapping. The dogs instantly bonded and spent the next thirty minutes playing with each other while the dog's owner Rick and I stood mostly silent, watching the energy and joy of dog play. It didn't take long before my daily routine included a visit to that park. As soon as the two dogs spotted each other, they were lost in their mutual love of being together.

I didn't speak to Rick much those first few days beyond a perfunctory "hi." But the infectious nature of the dogs' friendship wore away our natural shyness, and we learned to talk to each other—first about our dogs, but gradually about the rest of our lives.

By the next move my family made, I'd learned something about making friends by sharing what you have in common. Apollo also continued to be a bridge for me, helping me meet strangers and new people, even a few of my classmates. Having a dog didn't make me popular in school, but it seemed to make me more comfortable with myself. I was a much different kid my senior year in high school than I'd been a few years before. However, when we lost

Apollo just a year after I graduated, I was devastated. I was already feeling adrift, not knowing what to do with my life. And now I was also alone. Eventually, I stopped resisting Dad's encouragement to try the Army and took the plunge.

The routine of Army life gave me structure, and the opportunity to serve my country gave me purpose. I was almost excited when, after a few months, my platoon was deployed to Afghanistan to support Operation Freedom. Although the base was in a remote area that didn't get a lot of action, I enjoyed being in a new country and learning about its culture while also protecting the citizens of another country. But I continued to be lonely. I often walked the perimeter of the camp, thinking about how much Rick and Apollo had done to bring me out of my shell and wishing for the same kind of connection in this foreign place. I felt like I was swimming in a sea of potential friends but didn't know how to grab hold. I got my wish sooner than I could have hoped.

Just a few weeks after I was deployed, I found myself on midnight guard duty, which suited my solitary nature, but didn't make it any easier to make friends. My only company was Grant Miller, the other night guard, who seemed even shyer than me.

One night I was making rounds and munching on a sandwich when I heard a sound of distress from outside the gate, a sound almost like whimpering. Cautiously, I peeked my head around the wired gate and was shocked to find a scruffy-looking mutt staring straight at me, head tilted, tongue hanging out and tail thumping. The matted hair and protruding bones showed me he'd been in the wild for a long time, but he was friendly and his big brown eyes and whining made it seem like he'd come to the gate to ask my help. My heart melted, and I took a step just outside the gate not able to help myself. I gave the little guy my lunch, figuring he needed it more than I did.

Back in camp, I berated myself.

Geez, Steve. Animal 101…what do you think is going to happen if you give food to a starving dog?

I knew the little guy would be back, and I was right. He was there the next night and the night after that, and I recognized my colossal mistake. I couldn't keep a dog inside the base, but I hated thinking what was happening to the mutt during the day. Still, I just couldn't abandon my new friend. After a few nights, I took a chance and brought the dog into the guardhouse to meet Grant, and my second friendship in Afghanistan was born. Grant loved dogs as much as I did and missed the one he'd left back in the States. We spent the next several hours playing with the dog and talking to each other. At the end of duty that night, we were both enthralled and discussing what we might do with a stray in this harsh country. It was hard to usher him out the gate that night, but we knew we had to shoo him off. Nevertheless, the next night, about an hour after going on guard duty, the dog showed up at the gate again, plopped his rear down just outside of the guardhouse and patiently waited until we noticed. Grant and I bonded over what was now a mutual concern.

"What are we going to do, Grant? We can't keep an animal here."

"Maybe he'll just wander off some night and find a new place to go," Grant said. But we both knew it wouldn't happen. The dog had adopted me and now Grant the second the starved animal found friendly faces.

Every night the dog was waiting for us just outside the gate, and every day Grant or I were off duty, he found us the minute we left the compound. He followed us wherever we went, becoming a constant companion.

At least I now had a co-conspirator in Grant and together we came up with a plan: we'd keep the dog fed at night while we looked for its owner in the nearby village. While this plan started with just us two, the conspiracy gradually grew as we found other soldiers willing to help but keep their mouths shut that a dog was hanging around the post.

Meanwhile, my solitary existence was slowly dissolving. During the day, there were long walks with my new companion, exploring the areas around the base I knew were safe to walk, and wandering into town seeking the owner. My walking companion was a good listener and an even better observer.

I remember one day in particular when we were walking along and my new friend stopped dead and stared straight ahead. Naturally, I also stopped, wondering if danger was ahead. But when I looked where he was staring, I saw a herd of Ibex, grazing on what little grass they could find. I thought surely my friend would make a ruckus and go for those beasts, but he stood stock-still, apparently as wonder-filled as I was at this amazing sight. We stood for nearly ten minutes until the creatures wandered off. In all that time, the dog never made a peep.

Back in camp, I realized that not only had Grant and I had bonded over this dog and our mutual secret, I gradually was making other new friends with the men and women who were conspirators. The dog's presence was gradually accepted, and we found many volunteers willing to feed him or give him some attention. We even hid him away on a couple of nights when the temperatures were low.

Meanwhile, by searching for his owner, I also got to know the locals in town. Before my walks with the dog, I'd barely said more than a polite "hello" to any of the people in the area surrounding the base. With the dog in tow, I found that I became almost a local celebrity.

"Have you seen this dog before? Do you know who its owner is?" I said a hundred times. Those that understood the words simply shook their heads. Finally, one astute teenager simply replied: "You are owned *by* the dog."

That was the moment I realized he was right. I didn't want to find whatever owner had abandoned the poor mutt. The dog was mine and occasionally Grant's and sometimes our other friends. The base had become his home. I finally named him Charlie.

The routine of feeding him at night, walking with him outside the base during the day, and occasionally sneaking him onto the base for a snooze continued for the next six months. During that time, I also came to realize my feelings of being lost were gone. I had friends who helped me with Charlie. I had Grant who became a best buddy. I even had local townspeople who would give Charlie water or treats during our frequent strolls. As the days passed and my relationships deepened, I realized that the scruffy little Charlie was also extremely smart. And after one fateful day, I even received permission from my commander to include the dog on official patrols of the surrounding areas.

This day was clear and bright and Grant, Charlie and I walked along the border of a village. It was supposed to be a safe zone. But a flash of light and an explosion changed all that. In just a few moments, I saw the damage one bomb can do to a small village. Many of the buildings lay in a rubble, and I knew there was a chance some of the villagers were gone or hurt. One young woman came flying out of the fog of plaster and dirt, crying out for help. I understood enough to realize she believed her four-year-old child was buried under one of the building's remains. Grant and I leaped into action and radioed for backup from our fellow soldiers back at the post. When they arrived, a group of us began to clear away the spot where the woman had left her child, trying to locate the baby.

In the midst of the action, I noticed Charlie barking frantically, something that was unusual for him. I paused in my digging and went to calm him, only to have him move ten feet away and bark again. I followed him, and he repeated the action: barking loudly, then running further. Eventually, Charlie led me right to the child hiding in the woods, where he'd fled and remained, terrified to come out.

I have no idea how Charlie knew what we were looking for or where to look, but I was incredibly proud of him when I brought the boy back to his relieved and grateful mother. After that, Charlie became part of our base's regular patrols.

I didn't know, however, how deep his ability for heroism went until the fateful day I last saw him. I set out for my usual stroll, and he quickly found me and fell into lockstep as he often did. We played fetch and frolicked, delighting in the sun and each other. My last memory of that day was Charlie turning my way and suddenly leaping right at me.

I woke up three days later to find out I'd stepped on a landmine and had been evac'ed to a military hospital, where I eventually lost my right leg below the knee. For much of that time, I struggled to regain memories of the weeks leading up to the mine explosion. The nurses told me that the guard on gate duty had been approached by a frantic and badly wounded dog. The guard and a small detail found me lying just a hundred yards away in a field.

    I was sent home to recover before I even had a chance to find out what happened to Charlie. For the next six months, I concentrated on regaining the desire to live and learning how to move and walk again. Still, the desire to learn what happened to my hero never left me. I wrote to Grant, who had arrived back in the states almost a year after me and found out that, despite being gravely injured, Charlie had survived. To thank him, the post commander allowed him to remain within the post, cared for during his recovery by the friends I'd left behind. However, since the soldiers had begun returning home, those on the base had lost track of what happened to Charlie.

Luckily, I'm persistent, and I used every connection I'd made while overseas to find out that the mother of the child Charlie had saved had taken in her hero. I knew she'd done it for me: an extra mouth to feed was a burden in that village—she wanted to help as I'd helped her.

I knew, though, that I had to do something to pay back Charlie and help the woman and her family. But even more, Charlie belonged at my side. Although it took a lot of time, money and patience to get beyond the bureaucratic tape, my persistence paid off.

So here I am, standing at the gate, waiting for my Charlie. He's been given proper vaccinations, spent some time in quarantine and is finally about to be with me in America.

As I watch the passengers make their way past the gate, my thoughts turn to everything Charlie and I went through together. He literally saved my life, and much like Apollo, he helped make my life more complete by showing me a way to overcome my innate shyness.

He not only gave me his own love fully, he enabled me to embrace the love of others.

Suddenly, I notice a crowd murmuring near the gate, and I wonder if there is a problem. Before I can sort out what's happening, I see fur running toward me, a frantic security guard hard on the heels of my Charlie. The next thing I know, my face is soaking wet and my heart is full once again.

The authors

F. Sharon Swope is co-author of the mystery-romance books The Fate Series, as well as another collection of short stories *Holiday Connections*. Sharon ran her local hometown newspaper *The Edgerton Earth* with husband Robert W. Swope for many years and wrote a popular local column for that paper. She always wanted to write fiction, so at age eighty-two, she sat down at a computer and started writing The Fate Series. She is now ninety-one and still passionate about words.

Genilee Swope Parente is Sharon's co-author of The Fate Series and *Holiday Connections* as well as a writer/editor for *Relative Connections*. She has more than forty years of experience as a writer/editor and manager of magazines, newsletters and many other forms of the written word. The joy in her life, however, has been fiction writing. Parente is working on several books of her own.

Genilee is Sharon's second-born daughter.

Allyn M. Stotz has used the vivid imagination she was born with to create children's books. She has eight books published and many more in the works. She has also been published in several children's magazines. Allyn began writing in 2009 and had her first picture book *The Pea in Peanut Butter* published in 2011. You can find out more about Allyn and see her books at www.allynstotz.blogspot.com

Allyn is Sharon's third-born daughter.

Mark Swope's avid passion for words is spent pursuing fantasy/science fiction and suspense/mystery books. He has to fit reading around the pursuit of his first passion: music. Among the instruments Mark has taken up have been the euphonium, baritone saxophone and hammered dulcimer. When he's making money these days, it's for the U.S. Postal Service as an Operations Analyst. He's also contributed many stories to the USPS employee newsletter.

Mark is Sharon's son.

Christina Rae Parente is still determining how best to use her skills as a writer once she's out of college and not taking multiple creative writing classes. She spends some of her nose-in-a-book time these days reading about psychology as she continues the pursuit of a degree in that area. She's one of those students who has to have a job so she's worked in a pet store, been an office worker bee, managed a pizza branch, been a delivery driver, worked for Amazon and whatever else pays the bills.

Christina is Sharon's granddaughter.

Other books by F. Sharon Swope and Genilee Swope Parente:

The Fates Series:

An inheritance has allowed private investigator Sam Osborne to take on only the cases that appeal to his appetite for puzzles. Along with solutions to those mysteries, he finds clients who fall in love.

Twist of Fate

Wretched Fate

Violet Fate

Treasured Fate

Architect of Fate

Also by the authors:

Holiday Connections

Available at all online retail outlets.

www.swopeparente.com

www.ingramcontent.com/pod-product-compliance
Lightning Source LLC
Chambersburg PA
CBHW070758020526
44118CB00036B/1879